TRAINING FOR QUALITY

HIGH/SCOPE
EDUCATIONAL RESEARCH FOUNDATION
Ypsilanti, Michigan

*Monographs of the
High/Scope Educational Research Foundation
Number Nine*

TRAINING FOR QUALITY

Improving Early Childhood Programs Through Systematic Inservice Training

Ann S. Epstein

with a foreword by

Lilian G. Katz

THE HIGH/SCOPE PRESS

Published by
High/Scope® Press

A division of the
High/Scope Educational Research Foundation
600 North River Street
Ypsilanti, Michigan 48198-2898
(313)485-2000, FAX (313)485-0704

Marge Senninger, High/Scope Press Editor

Linda Eckel, Cover and Text Design
Margaret FitzGerald, Production

Library of Congress Cataloging-in-Publication Data

Epstein, Ann S.
   Training for quality : improving early childhood programs through systematic inservice training / Ann S. Epstein ; with a foreword by Lilian G. Katz.
      p. cm. – (Monographs of the High/Scope Educational Research Foundation ; no. 9)
   Includes bibliographical references
   ISBN 0-929816-56-0 : $19.00
   1. Early childhood teachers–In-service training–United States–Longitudinal studies. 2. Early childhood education–United States–Longitudinal studies. I. Title. II. Series.
LB1732.3.E67   1993
371.1'46–dc20
                                                                    93-8514
                                                                       CIP

Printed in the United States of America

Contents

Tables and Figures

Tables

Figures

Acknowledgments

A project as complex as the series of inservice training studies reported here necessarily entails the efforts and cooperation of many people. The very idea for the research originated with David Weikart taking High/Scope inservice training "to scale." His vision of a national early childhood training initiative, implemented by High/Scope staff consultants and endorsed High/Scope trainers throughout the country, spurred us to ask the crucial questions about the range and effectiveness of their training activities.

Once we began to ask the questions, we needed the resources to undertake a multifaceted and comprehensive evaluation. The research would not have been possible without the support of the Ford Foundation and our project officer, Shelby Miller. In funding both the training projects and the evaluation, the Ford Foundation operationalized a commitment to upgrade the quality of early childhood programs, based on sound principles of program development and a defensible research base. With the anticipated growth of early childhood programs in the coming years, we need more such commitments to evaluating and informing our efforts throughout the expansion process.

Research plans and funding are a beginning, but it takes action to turn ideas into reality. This project was fortunate to have a team of four people who made the research happen. Polly Neill and Karen Parsell had major responsibility for identifying the sample, recruiting the data collectors, and monitoring and coordinating all of the data collection activities across the country. Shannan McNair and Peggy Wilson helped to adapt the observational instruments and trained and supervised all of the observers; their vigilance assured the data's thoroughness and validity. Over its lifetime, every project has its moments of euphoria and its instances of crisis. With great good humor, resourcefulness, and appreciation for one another, we rode this roller coaster together. Some work experiences stand out in the memories of a career; I believe this project will be one of them.

The excellent recruitment and training strategies of the project team produced a highly qualified corps of data collectors, who observed hundreds of programs across the country, conducted interviews with trainers and teachers, and observed and assessed young children in a variety of program settings. For their persistence and diligence, special thanks are extended to the observers and interviewers in this study: Mary Achatz, Susan Brao, Nancy Brown, Lisa Cameron, Lisa Canning, Jill Claxton, Linda Ehrstine, Catherine Farrell, Sandy Fisher, Nancy Greenleaf, Diane Heinrich, Rita Khoutieff, Michele LaClair, Shannon Lockhart, Maria Martin, Sharon Massman, Leslie McAdoo, Anita Newton, Marilyn Rie, Gail Rigelhaupt, Brenlee Robinson, Nancy Rosenthal, Sharon Shelton, Cadey Sontag, Linda West, Alberta Williams, and Tracy Williams.

Pinpointing the people who contribute ideas is more elusive than identifying those who enact them. Nevertheless, certain colleagues at High/Scope stand out for their role in developing this project's conceptual base. In the Research Division, Lawrence Schweinhart and Mary Larner helped to design the study. Mary Larner also directed the Registry survey, and

Lawrence Schweinhart was a constant sounding board throughout the writing and revision of the book. Other research colleagues who deserve thanks are Molly Gong, for doing the data analysis, and Sherri Oden, for reviewing the manuscript. John Wilson assisted with the Registry survey and the ethnographic observations during his year at the Foundation. Several staff members in the Program and Development Services divisions also contributed their voices to the review and interpretation of the findings, most notably Philip Hawkins, Mary Hohmann, Clay Shouse, Sue Terdan, and Mark Tompkins.

Support staff at High/Scope also played a crucial role in the research activities and publication of this book. Kay Long supervised a data processing team that included Andra Bostian, Susan Brao, Nancy Burandt, George Claxton, Elaine Hovey, and Cadey Sontag. Steve McHugh was responsible for project mailings and for duplicating multiple copies of the manuscript during the internal and external review process. Final editing of the manuscript was the responsibility of Marge Senninger. Diana Knepp assisted her by preparing the text for typesetting and by typesetting the many tables that accompany the text. The book's design and production were the work of Linda Eckel and Margaret FitzGerald, respectively.

The project received additional intellectual capital and encouragement from the members of its advisory panel: Carollee Howes, Mary Kennedy, Sam Meisels, and the late Joe Stephens. They contributed their expertise in the areas of teacher training, early childhood program development, and program and child assessment. Lilian Katz, one of the most thoughtful and respected leaders in the field, graciously agreed to write the Foreword for the book. Other outside reviewers whose comments helped to strengthen this report included Frank Blackwell, Paula Jorde Bloom, Sue Bredecamp, Linda Espinosa, Jenni Klein, Joan Lombardi, Gwen Morgan, Barbara Willer, and Janice Molnar, who took over as the Ford Foundation project officer in the latter stages of the manuscript's preparation. All of these individuals helped the team at High/Scope to broaden our focus and to consider training issues of national importance from a variety of evaluation and policy perspectives.

Finally, this research owes its gratitude to those for whom the quality of early childhood programs is a matter of daily commitment and concern. Special thanks are extended to the administrators and teachers who welcomed us into their programs and to the parents and children who cooperated with our data collection. It is ultimately for these individuals, whose lives revolve around the delivery and use of early childhood services, that this research was undertaken. We hope its optimistic message—that good inservice training can produce high-quality programs—will help to shape the direction of early childhood policies and practices in the coming decades.

Foreword

With the Training of Trainers Evaluation reported in this monograph, the High/Scope Educational Research Foundation once again advances the field of early childhood education. This study—the first of its kind—examines the link between inservice training and program implementation and assesses the ultimate impact of both on children's development. The study's subjects were drawn from a sufficient diversity of communities, program settings, families, and children to lend confidence to the findings. Indeed, the very words of the trainers and teachers involved in the evaluation reveal that most of them confront the same range of issues faced by a large proportion of their colleagues in other early childhood programs across the country.

Thus this research, though specifically examining High/Scope's unique approach to training teachers and teaching children, provides many basic lessons about the characteristics of effective support and inservice education for all early childhood educators.

Lessons About Inservice Training

First, to make a real difference in teaching practices, inservice training has to be available on the site. In this way, the trainers can be readily accessible to teachers for consultation and support. Inservice training is also most likely to be effective when those responsible for it know well the community, the school, and even the children of the teachers they wish to help.

Second, inservice training should be continuous and constant rather than made up of the one-shot, conference presentations and lectures that are characteristic of so many inservice and staff-development programs. To achieve this goal of continuity and constancy, High/Scope has prepared and endorsed large numbers of trainers of teachers in communities across the United States and in other countries where the High/Scope Curriculum has been adopted.

Third, teacher training is most likely to be effective when it is based on a coherent conception of teaching and learning. The High/Scope Curriculum, developed over a long period of experimentation and implementation, presents trainers, teachers, and parents with a comprehensive, well-articulated view of how children learn and what they should be learning. Unless the curriculum to be adopted is so clearly formulated, teachers have few ways of knowing when their implementation is successful and when corrections and modifications are needed.

Fourth, the study results support the principle that the way adults are trained should be congruent with the way they in turn are to teach. The trainers implementing the High/Scope inservice model exemplify in their own behavior the same approach to teaching and learning that their trainees are expected to use in their subsequent work with adults and children. Consistent with the High/Scope Curriculum for children, the inservice training model emphasizes (a) learning as active and interactive rather than as passive and reactive, (b) individual support for learners, and (c) responsiveness to the range of differences in characteristics and needs of those being trained. In sum, like the High/Scope Curriculum for children, the strategies employed by the trainers of trainers, and in turn by the trainers of teachers, are developmentally appropriate.

Fifth, as teachers must with children, the trainers of teachers accepted and accommodated to the fact that it often takes a long time for genuine and lasting learning to occur. Effective inservice education requires time and continuity, because it addresses teachers' ideas, beliefs, and dispositions, as well as their skills and techniques.

Finally, the findings tell us that providing an optimal environment for children is related to providing an optimal environment for adults who work with them. The fact that teachers in this study saw as important not only salaries and benefits but also other aspects of the interpersonal relationships in the setting confirms the importance of providing good working conditions for those who need to work effectively with children.

Provocative Findings

The evaluation raises a number of important questions to be addressed by the early childhood profession. For example, what are the implications of the finding that in the study's sample of teachers, teaching experience, inservice training, and program quality were more strongly related to children's learning and development than was formal preservice training? Does this mean that we must ask questions about the nature of preservice training? Do all or just some kinds of preservice training for teachers seem to have little effect on the development of children? When choices have to be made about the allocation of scarce resources and funding for training, should inservice training claim a very high priority?

With this comprehensive evaluation, the High/Scope Foundation offers a model for maximizing limited resources: The evaluation bears witness that through careful training, 1,075 trainers were able to multiply their effectiveness, making their knowledge and skills available to roughly 26,000 teachers working directly with over a quarter of a million children a year! A report such as this provides us with many ideas to help strengthen the quality of early childhood programs as they continue to expand in the foreseeable future.

LILIAN G. KATZ
Professor of Early Childhood Education
Director of ERIC Clearinghouse on Elementary
and Early Childhood Education
University of Illinois—Urbana

EXECUTIVE SUMMARY

The High/Scope
Training of Trainers Evaluation

The Training of Trainers (ToT) Evaluation investigated the efficacy of the High/Scope training and curriculum models for improving the quality of early childhood programs on a national scale. In 1981, the High/Scope Educational Research Foundation in Ypsilanti, Michigan, embarked on the Training of Trainers initiative to provide inservice training to large numbers of early childhood practitioners throughout the country. As of 1991, we had conducted 80 ToT projects, producing 1,075 endorsed High/Scope trainers in 38 states and 12 other countries. These 1,075 trainers had in turn trained an estimated 26,000 teachers working with over a quarter of a million children annually.

Between 1989 and 1992 we conducted a multimethod evaluation to examine the effectiveness of the chain of transmission from the High/Scope consultant to the endorsed agency trainer to teachers to children. As part of this ambitious undertaking, we collected anecdotal records from the consultants and the 793 participants in 40 ToT projects, surveyed a random sample of 203 endorsed High/Scope trainers around the country, interviewed and observed teachers in 244 High/Scope and 122 non-High/Scope settings, and assessed 97 children in High/Scope and 103 children in comparison programs.

In addition to the specific question of whether High/Scope's training is effective, the evaluation study also addressed the broader question of how inservice training can improve early childhood program quality and enhance young children's development. Does inservice training, over and above a teacher's preservice education and experience, improve the teacher's ability to deliver an appropriate and challenging program to young children? Does this training result in recognizable benefits for the children? And if it *is* possible to improve program quality and child outcomes, then what have we learned about *how* training can be structured to bring about these positive results?

The study provided a strongly affirmative answer to the first question: High/Scope training does work. We found program sites around the country, separated from the High/Scope Foundation by both time and distance, to be implementing the High/Scope Curriculum at impressive levels of fidelity and quality. High/Scope sites significantly outscored comparison sites on a developmentally based index of program quality. Children in High/Scope programs significantly outscored those in comparison programs on measures of developmental progress.

The research also provided strong evidence for the general assertion that inservice training can contribute significantly to program quality and children's development. On-the-job training continues the process of professional development after formal education ceases. On-site learning helps teachers convert experience into improved practice, thereby enhancing program quality. And better program quality in turn facilitates sound child development.

The question that remains is this: How can the early childhood field use this knowledge about the effectiveness of inservice training? Following is a summary of what we learned from the ToT Evaluation and of how this information can be used to improve the quality of early childhood programs throughout the country.

Summary of Study Procedures

The High/Scope ToT Evaluation investigated the dissemination model with three related studies that each examined one part of the chain of transmission from High/Scope consultants to endorsed trainers to teachers to children:

1. The Trainer Study addressed the first link of the chain—transmission from consultant to trainers. To provide insights into the training experience and its immediate effects on participating agencies, the study began with a *process analysis* of the consultants and the 793 endorsement candidates from 40 ToT projects. We explored the consultants' and candidates' perspectives on ToT by analyzing the journals, debriefings, and final evaluation forms completed during the training. A *Registry*[1] *survey* then examined what a national random sample of 203 High/Scope endorsed trainers actually did in the months and years after their ToT projects ended. The survey determined the amount and nature of training that took place in the trainers' agencies as they disseminated the High/Scope model.

2. The Teacher Study looked at the second link—transmission from trainer to teachers—by examining inservice training from the teachers' perspective and by investigating the impact of inservice training on program practices. A sample of 244 High/Scope and 122 comparison teachers from California, Michigan, and New York participated in extensive *teacher interviews* that asked about their backgrounds, their program philosophies, and the inservice training at their agencies. We also conducted *program observations* using three measures of program quality: the Arnett Global Rating Scale, the Early Childhood Environment Rating Scale (ECERS), and the High/Scope Program Implementation Profile (PIP). At a very basic level, we asked whether training was associated with higher levels of program quality. Did the High/Scope training result in teachers who implemented good early childhood practices? Compared with teachers who did not receive High/Scope inservice training, did High/Scope-trained teachers offer better quality programs?

---

[1]The High/Scope Registry is the official listing of those who have received High/Scope endorsement. The *High/Scope Registry 1989 Directory*, used in the study reported here, contained the names of endorsed preschool trainers. Subsequently, the Registry has grown to include endorsed movement and dance trainers. Beginning in 1993, the Registry will also list certified teachers and programs.

3. The Child Study examined the last link in the chain—transmission from teacher to children. We assessed 97 children attending High/Scope programs and 103 children in comparison settings, using two measures: The Developmental Indicators for the Assessment of Learning—Revised (DIAL-R) screening test and the High/Scope Child Observation Record (COR) for Ages 2½–6. Analyses examined the impact of teachers' inservice training and actual implementation on the development of young children. We also investigated differences in children who attended High/Scope versus comparison programs.

Summary of Study Results

What We Learned From the Trainer Study

What did candidates gain from their participation in ToT projects?

- A comprehensive theoretical framework for organizing beliefs and practices

- An enhanced understanding of appropriate practices and strategies for adult learning and children's development

- A professional network of colleagues with compatible philosophies

- A renewed dedication to improving the quality of early childhood programs

Who were High/Scope endorsed trainers in the 1989 Registry survey?

- Endorsed trainers were highly educated and experienced in early childhood:

  88 percent had undergraduate degrees; 51 percent had graduate-level degrees.

  70 percent had early childhood degrees or credentials; 60 percent had both college and early childhood training.

  94 percent had worked in the field for over 5 years; 75 percent, for more than 10 years.

- Endorsed trainers worked in a variety of early childhood program settings:

  50 percent worked in Head Start.

  27 percent worked in public schools.

  21 percent worked in private nonprofit programs, including both center-based and home-based settings.

  2 percent worked in private for-profit programs.

How much and what kinds of training did endorsed trainers provide to teachers?

- Trainers worked with an average of 25 teachers in 12 to 13 classrooms.

- Trainers spent an average of 8 hours per week training staff.

- Trainers on average provided the following:

    One large-group presentation annually to introduce the curriculum to staff

    Monthly hands-on workshops for small groups of staff members

    Monthly classroom visits to conduct observation and feedback

    Three informal classroom visits each month to monitor implementation

- As of 1991, 1,075 trainers had trained an estimated 26,000 teachers working with over a quarter of a million children annually in 13,000 programs. Trainers rated nearly 6,000 (45 percent) of these programs as demonstration-level quality.

- To date, High/Scope has reached 6 percent of potential early childhood training professionals overall, including 12.5 percent of those serving low-income children.

What We Learned From the Teacher Study

Who were the teachers in the study?

- Teachers in both the High/Scope and the comparison agencies in this study were highly qualified in terms of education and experience:

    Nearly 70 percent had 4-year college degrees; over 70 percent had early childhood degrees or credentials; over half (52 percent) had both college and early childhood training. They averaged more than 10 years of experience in the field.

- Teachers in this study represented the top 20 percent of the early childhood profession in terms of background and qualifications.

Did inservice training differ for teachers in High/Scope and comparison agencies?

- Significantly more High/Scope than comparison agencies provided inservice training (94 percent versus 84 percent) and required attendance at training (79 percent versus 59 percent).[2]

- Teachers in High/Scope versus teachers in comparison programs, to a significant degree,

    Attended more workshops given by in-house trainers

---

[2]In this study, results are reported as significant at $p < .05$, two-tailed. Results that are significant at $.05 < p < .10$ are reported as trends when they are corroborated by two or more findings on different measures.

Received more classroom visits from trainers

Spent more training sessions covering curriculum issues, teaching practices, and child assessment

Participated more actively in training

Were more open to changing teaching practices, based on inservice training

Did program quality differ in High/Scope and comparison agencies?

- Teachers in both groups offered good programs, but on overall quality, High/Scope programs were rated significantly higher than comparison programs.

- Observers rated teachers in High/Scope programs significantly higher than teachers in comparison programs on these practices:

  Organizing and labeling the room to promote children's independence

  Providing many materials that were easily accessible to children

  Promoting multicultural awareness

  Encouraging children to choose and carry out activities based on their interests

  Encouraging children to reflect on their actions and experiences

  Using observations and open-ended questions to extend children's play

- Observers rated comparison programs significantly higher than High/Scope programs on supporting children's gross-motor development.

Did inservice training improve program quality?

- The types of inservice training provided by High/Scope endorsed trainers—curriculum workshops and classroom visits by in-house trainers—were positively and significantly associated with program quality.

- Teachers' education, experience, and inservice training were all highly significant predictors of program quality.

- Inservice training obtained in the context of a good program environment can provide the role models and support needed for professional development.

What We Learned From the Child Study

Who were the children in the study?

- Children in the total sample (composed of comparable and equally diverse High/Scope and comparison groups) were

  Aged 2½–6 years, with an average age of 4.4 years

43 percent white, 32 percent black, 25 percent other

From Head Start (46 percent), public school (19 percent), and nonprofit (35 percent) agencies

From urban, suburban, and rural settings

Were there developmental differences between children in High/Scope and children in comparison programs?

- Children in High/Scope programs significantly outperformed children in comparison programs in the following areas:

  Initiative, including complex play, joining in program activities

  Social relations, including relating to peers, social problem-solving

  Motor development, including music and movement, focusing energies during physical activities

  Overall development

- Children in High/Scope programs tended to outscore children in comparison programs on the following:

  Cognitive development, including representation, classification, and language skills

- Comparison children showed no significant advantages over High/Scope children on any of the child assessments.

Did inservice training and program quality affect children's development?

- Teachers' experience and inservice training, but not their formal education, were significant predictors of children's development.

- Program quality was a significant predictor of children's development:

  Access to diverse materials and opportunities for planning and recall were the two most important dimensions of program quality for children.

  Children's language and creative representational skills were the two areas most strongly affected by program quality.

Conclusions and Implications

Preparing a National Cadre of Early Childhood Trainers

Systematic leadership training can prepare a trainers' corps, national in scope, capable of disseminating a body of early childhood theory and practice to staff.

- The investment in training will result in improved program practices and enhanced child outcomes at an expanding rate.

- Members of the corps will remain committed to continuing their training activities over a period of many years.

- The dissemination chain will expand at a ratio of 1 trainer to 25 teachers serving 250 children per year.

  There are currently 7.3 million 3- and 4-year-olds in the United States, and 4.5 million (61.4 percent) of them are in early childhood programs.

  Based on the above ratio, we would need to prepare a national corps of 18,000 trainers to reach every teacher and every child in a program.

  If all 1.6 million poor 3- and 4-year-olds were to be served in Head Start or other subsidized programs, a corps of 6,400 trainers could insure that high-quality programs produce a return on the public investment.

Methods for preparing a trainers' corps can be effective if they embody these principles of active learning for adults:

- An intense immersion in the training process

- Opportunities to integrate theory and practice, based on a coherent framework

- A dual emphasis on adult learning and children's development

- Opportunities for trainers to network and appreciate their significance as part of a larger national (or international) initiative

- Strategies for addressing the organizational change process

- Follow-up training—inservice for trainers themselves—to continue the process of learning and disseminating the curriculum

Agencies can enhance the work of corps members by providing the following features of organizational support:

- Institutional commitment to the professional development of teaching staff through ongoing inservice training.

- Resources to maintain a trainer as an in-house staff-development specialist, to provide continuity and consistency in training.

- Job description that includes training responsibilities as an explicit role. Trainers may fulfill other functions, as long as a significant portion of their work time is specifically allocated to training activities.

Providing Inservice Training That Improves Teaching Practices

Inservice training can make a good program even better.

- Good programs provide safe and well-equipped physical environments monitored by nurturing adults.

- Inservice training results in better programs that also provide these features:

    Improved access to materials

    More opportunities for children to exercise choice

    Extended sequences allowing children to initiate, carry out, and review their own activities

    Enhanced observational and questioning skills that enable adults to support children's reasoning and language development

Inservice training, as a supplement to education or experience, is an effective option for further improving program quality.

- The benefits of teachers' formal education are enhanced by inservice training.

- Experience will not improve teaching skills unless it is accompanied by inservice training in the context of a good program.

- Inservice training targeted at top-level teachers is an effective strategy for upgrading professional skills at all staff levels.

    Trained teachers establish good learning-environments for colleagues.

    Training allows experienced teachers to mentor less experienced peers.

Inservice training improves teaching practices if it includes the following:

- Workshops, presented by in-house trainers, with an emphasis on active participation by adults

- Specific coverage of curriculum issues and teaching practices

- Classroom visits to observe and give feedback to teachers as they turn ideas into practice

- Follow-up sessions that encourage staff to share problems and solutions

Implementing Programs That Enhance the Development of Young Children

Children's development is enhanced by programs that provide access to diverse materials and offer opportunities for planning and recall.

- High-quality programs provide children with ready access to a broad range of creative materials. Children benefit when they are encouraged to manipulate diverse materials in activities of their own choosing.

- High-quality programs provide opportunities for children to plan, carry out, and review their activities in a supportive context. This sequence promotes independent problem-solving, social cooperation, and language development.

Children's development is enhanced by programs that also support adult development.

- When agencies make a commitment to teachers through tangible rewards and ongoing professional development, teachers make a commitment to children.

- If they are given the freedom to learn experientially, teachers extend this same freedom to the children in their programs.

––––––––––

Discourse about early childhood programs should no longer be limited to issues of availability and access. Program quality is now a permanent fixture in the national debate. Developing appropriate curriculum models—and preparing staff to deliver their essential ingredients—are the keys to achieving the standards inherent in high-quality programs. The High/Scope ToT Evaluation has contributed in a major way to our understanding of what defines program quality. And most important, it has documented the viability of systematic and coherent inservice training for disseminating quality throughout the early childhood community.

It is now up to everyone in the field—classroom teachers, home day care providers, parents, agency administrators, and policymakers from the local to the national level—to convert these lessons into action. We know that inservice training can work on a large scale, and we know what elements are crucial to making it work at the individual-program level. If we are concerned about the professional development of a growing segment of our labor force, and if we are concerned about the quality of the services they deliver to our nation's young children, then we must find the resources to invest in training for quality.

TRAINING FOR QUALITY

I Introduction and Overview

The High/Scope Training of Trainers (ToT) Evaluation asks whether systematic inservice training is an effective strategy for improving the quality of early childhood programs in America. To address this question, the Foundation undertook an ambitious multimethod evaluation that collected anecdotal records from the consultants and 793 participants in 40 ToT projects, surveyed 203 endorsed High/Scope trainers around the country, interviewed and observed teachers in 366 High/Scope and non-High/Scope settings, and assessed 200 children attending High/Scope and comparison programs.

Why This Study at This Time

Over a decade ago, High/Scope embarked on the Training of Trainers program, an initiative to provide inservice training to large numbers of early childhood practitioners throughout the country. This endeavor has encompassed both a *training model* for working with adults and a *curriculum model* for working with children. Because of High/Scope's visibility in the early childhood field and because of the potential reach of High/Scope's dissemination activities, the Foundation recognizes its responsibility to validate its training efforts.

This sense of responsibility is what spurred the undertaking of the multimethod ToT evaluation. To date, no other study has taken such a comprehensive look at the processes and outcomes of inservice training. We have examined each step, from the preparation of trainers to their training activities with teachers, from the behavior of teachers in the program setting to the program effects on young children's development.

Between 1981 and 1991, High/Scope consultants conducted 80 ToT projects participated in by 1,500 prospective trainers from 38 states and 12 foreign countries. More ToT projects are currently under way.

As of 1991, 1,075 ToT participants had successfully completed training and become High/Scope *endorsed trainers*.[3] As such, they are now preparing thousands of professionals and paraprofessionals to implement the High/Scope Preschool Curriculum in a wide variety of program settings. Through its use of this multiplicative model, High/Scope has become one of the largest providers of early childhood inservice training in the United States.

Now, with a critical mass of trained practitioners to draw on, the Foundation is in a position to ask *if* its training and curriculum models are being faithfully implemented and *what effects* these models have on adults and children. Answering these basic questions is the intent and scope of the series of studies composing the ToT Evaluation reported here.

---

[3]Of all ToT participants over the decade 1981–1991, approximately 72 percent are registered as endorsed trainers. For projects in the last 5 years of the decade, the endorsement rate is 83 percent (see Chapter 3). Given improvements in recruitment, assessment, and record-keeping procedures, 83 percent is the more accurate and current statistic.

Early Childhood Programs in the Public Eye

Early childhood programs have entered the popular and political conscious-
ness of our country. Debates about who will provide these programs and
how they will be financed are regularly featured in the media. Beyond the
rhetoric and reasoned arguments, we must face the basic question: What
will make these programs *good* for the young children we entrust to them?
The quality of these programs is of central importance in the debate. Long-
term studies consistently demonstrate that only high-quality early
childhood programs have an enduring effect on the participants' lives.

Recent federal funding attests to the priority of early childhood programs on the national agenda:

- The budget for Head Start has increased nearly 80 percent in the last
  3 years. With the program currently operating at $2.2 billion, the next
  round of increases will be the largest since Head Start was created in
  1965. Funding for 1994 could be substantially higher.

- The Child Care and Development Block Grant provided states with
  $732 million for early childhood initiatives in 1991.

- Child Care Tax Credits will free up an average of $3.8 billion a year for
  the child care needs of low-income parents.

- The Family Support Act authorizes $300 million a year in child care
  payments for welfare-dependent families.

Private foundations are also promoting early childhood education. For
example, a recent national survey of kindergarten teachers by the Carnegie
Foundation for the Advancement of Teaching (1991) indicated that 1.5 million children (35 percent) are not ready to learn when they enter school.
This finding prompted Dr. Ernest Boyer, the Carnegie Foundation's presi-
dent, to recommend the following steps:

- Congress should designate Head Start as an entitlement program, with
  full funding for all eligible children and families by 1995.

- Every school district in the nation should establish preschool programs
  as an optional service for all 3- and 4-year-olds not served by Head
  Start.

- By the year 2000, states should adopt universal licensing standards
  based on the recommendations of a National Council on Child Care
  Standards.

- Every state should establish a preschool division in the governor's
  office to coordinate services.

- Every community college should establish an associate's degree (2-year)
  called *Child Care Professional*.

As these recommendations make clear, simply expanding the *number*
of early childhood programs is insufficient; responsible citizens must also
talk about the *quality* of these programs. And the public as a whole, and

policymakers and professionals in particular, must seek effective ways to build and maintain this program quality.

Inservice Training as a Prelude to Quality

Program quality, according to Caldwell and Hilliard (1985), depends first and foremost on staff quality, especially the quality of teachers and providers who are responsible for children's daily program experiences. A review of the research shows that the quality of staff, in turn, depends on the quality of their training (Phillips, 1987). Staff training may be of two types: preservice and inservice. This evaluation is concerned primarily with the nature of *inservice* training as conducted by High/Scope endorsed trainers who have completed ToT projects. Specifically, we asked ourselves, Could we contribute to the growing body of empirical evidence that inservice training results in better early childhood programs? Could we establish that the High/Scope model is an effective system for delivering this training?

For several reasons, identifying effective methods for providing inservice training on a large scale is critical to the early childhood field. The most compelling reason is that preservice training alone cannot keep up with the increased demand for early childhood staff. The Bureau of Labor Statistics has projected that by the year 2000, the demand for child care workers will grow by at least 20 percent, and the demand for preschool teachers, by at least 36 percent (Willer & Johnson, 1989). Obviously, community colleges and other facilities are not prepared to train such a large cadre of care providers within this short time-frame. High turnover rates contribute to the immediate shortage of trained and available staff.

Staff already working in the early childhood field have urgent training needs, as well. Since early childhood credentials from preservice training are often not required for entry-level teaching and provider positions (Morgan, 1987), many practitioners come to the field with unrelated backgrounds and varying levels of general work experience. Furthermore, many of the existing staff who *do* have preservice early childhood training find their training to be insufficient or outdated in light of current needs. As Lilian Katz (1979) has said,

> The timing of training should be shifted so that more training is available to the teacher *on* the job than *before* it. Many teachers say that their preservice education has had only a minor influence on what they do day-to-day in their classrooms, which suggests that strategies acquired before employment will often not be retrieved under pressure of concurrent forces and factors in the actual job situation (p. 12).

Knowledge about the components of good developmentally based early childhood programs has grown enormously in the past decade (e.g., Bredekamp, 1987; Epstein, Morgan, Curry, Endsley, Bradbard, & Rashid, 1985; Kontos & Stevens, 1985; Mitchell, 1988; National Association for the Education of Young Children, 1984b). Also, the populations served by early childhood programs are changing as the demographic composition of our society shifts with regard to income levels, racial and ethnic background, cultural and linguistic heritage (Kahn & Kamerman, 1987; Zigler & Lang, 1991).

Defining Good Inservice Training

Clearly, in this time of rapid progress and change, preparing early childhood teachers to deliver good programs must fall largely to inservice training methods. But too many early childhood programs, hampered by limited time and budget, offer no or minimal inservice training. This assertion is based on High/Scope's extensive training experience and corroborated by other trainers in the field (Bloom, Sheerer, Richard, & Britz, 1991). In some agencies, new staff may receive only a brief orientation regarding basic program policies and procedures. Even when programs do provide regular inservice training, they typically offer several training presentations on disconnected topics. Thus the training sessions may fail to have a lasting impact on staff knowledge and skills owing to the following drawbacks:

- Topics are not connected in any logical or cumulative fashion.

- Disconnected topics often mean a series of one-time presenters, and their methods of presentation may not be geared toward adult learning styles.

- The information presented by trainers is not related to a curriculum or program philosophy, and it is not connected to daily program practices. Consequently, staff may emerge with a few interesting ideas, but since they cannot readily fit them into the context of the overall program goals, there is no motivation to implement the ideas in any sustained manner.

- Theory is not accompanied by practical information. Staff are given no "how-to" guidelines for applying what they have learned.

- Discovery and application are disconnected. There is no natural cycle that alternates learning new ideas and trying them out in an interactive process over time.

- Follow-up is absent. The real questions surface when staff attempt to implement what they have learned. With no forum for addressing their questions to individuals or groups, staff do not receive the ongoing help they need to apply the lessons of inservice training.

The following characteristic features of the High/Scope approach to inservice training stand in direct contrast to these typical drawbacks:

- *Integrated content.* Inservice training follows a progression of interrelated topics, resulting in knowledge that is cumulative over the course of training.

- *Presentation geared to adult learning.* Training procedures are based on current knowledge about how adults learn. Trainers interact with teachers during group workshop presentations and make individual on-site visits to the classroom for observation and feedback.

- *Articulated curriculum.* High/Scope has a coherent curriculum model based on child development principles. The curriculum serves as a framework for applying and implementing new knowledge.

- *Hands-on practice.* Inservice training sessions explore strategies for practical application. Strategies are then practiced in the actual work setting.

- *Distributive learning.* Training is spread out over many months, so staff alternate one week of workshop sessions with several weeks of application at their sponsoring agency. This cycle promotes adaptation and problem solving, and it highlights the progression of skills over time.

- *Follow-up mechanisms.* The regularity of training and supervision means that follow-up opportunities are built into the model. Trainees can explore issues individually with their trainer, as well as in group sessions with their peers.

Evaluating the High/Scope National Inservice Training Model

The ToT Evaluation tests the validity of this High/Scope model for inservice training and curriculum implementation. It asks the question, Is the High/Scope method an effective strategy for meeting the national demand for well-trained early childhood staff and high-quality programs?

This basic question is addressed by the following three interrelated studies that make up the evaluation. Each study examines one part of the chain of transmission from High/Scope consultants to endorsed trainers to teachers to children. [See also Table 2, Design of the High/Scope Training of Trainers (ToT) Evaluation (1989–1992), later in this chapter.]

- *The Trainer Study* addresses the first link of the chain—transmission from consultant to trainer. It begins with a *process analysis*, to explore what it is like to participate in a High/Scope ToT project. This consists of analyzing the documented perspectives of candidates and consultants from 40 ToT projects, to gain insight into the training experience and its immediate effects on participating agencies. A *Registry*[4] *survey* then examines what endorsed trainers actually do in the months and years after their ToT projects end. The survey determines the amount and nature of training that takes place in their agencies as they disseminate the High/Scope model.

- *The Teacher Study* looks at the second link—transmission from trainer to teachers—by examining inservice training from the teachers' perspective and by examining training's impact on program practices. At a very basic level, we ask whether training is associated with higher levels of program quality. Does the High/Scope training result in teachers who implement good early childhood practices? Do these teachers offer better quality programs than are offered by those who do not receive High/Scope inservice training?

---

[4]The High/Scope Registry is the official listing of those who have received High/Scope endorsement. The *High/Scope Registry 1989 Directory*, used in the study reported here, contained the names of endorsed preschool trainers. Subsequently, the Registry has grown to include endorsed movement and dance trainers. Beginning in 1993, the Registry will also list certified teachers and programs.

- *The Child Study* examines the last link in the chain—transmission from teacher to children. An evaluation of inservice training is complete only if we look at the resulting practice and its effect on children. We must ask, What is the impact of teachers' inservice training and actual implementation on the development of young children? Are there differences in children who attend High/Scope versus comparison programs?

Relevant Issues in Training and Supporting Early Childhood Staff

To identify the factors that contribute significantly to teaching ability and program quality, research and theory have explored several avenues. One line of work compares the effects of *training* versus *experience* on the quality of teachers' caregiving behaviors. On the subject of training itself, there has been an attempt to tease out the methods that are most effective in transmitting appropriate developmental practices. Finally, another set of literature looks beyond the teachers to discover how the workplace itself affects job satisfaction and performance. In the following section, these three avenues of thought and investigation are explored.

Effects of Training and Experience

Examination of the background variables that affect caregiving behavior have focused primarily on two types of comparisons: training versus on-the-job experience, and overall level of formal education versus specific, child-related training.

Training versus experience   The popular myth that anyone who has experience raising or working with children can be a good child care provider is not supported by systematic research. Both the National Day Care Study (Ruopp, Travers, Glantz, Coelen, & Smith, 1979) and the National Child Care Staffing Study (Whitebook, Howes, & Phillips, 1989) "found job experience to hold little value as a route to good caregiving" (Whitebook, Howes, & Phillips, 1990, p. 40). Instead, formal education and specialized college-level early childhood training were the most significant predictors of job performance.

General versus specific training   Studies attempting to compare the effects of overall level of education versus specific child-related training are often inconclusive because educational levels are confounded by race and social class (Phillips, 1987). Despite methodological limitations, the evidence indicates that training specifically related to child development and the care of young children is an essential component of effective practice (Powell & Stremmel, 1989; Snider & Fu, 1990). Moreover, the specific training is most effective when it is job-related (Benham, Miller, & Kontos, 1988). Olson

(1990, p. 20) concluded: "Research suggests that there should be more of a continuum between a teacher's preservice and inservice training, and that many things learned on campus would be better learned on the job."

Characteristics of Effective Training Programs

Practice Current training models employ a sequence that runs counter to how most people learn: Theory comes at the outset, and practice comes only after theoretical coursework is completed. However, the notion that instruction must *be accompanied by* practical experience and hands-on application is receiving increasing support in the teacher-training literature (Jones, 1986; Katz, 1984). Moreover, there is some movement toward shifting the practicum to the earlier stages of preservice training. These trends are based on the growing realization that theory becomes meaningful and useful only when it is connected to experience. "The understanding of theory grows out of experience. The academic tradition has tried to reverse this direction, teaching theory before permitting any doing. The outcome has been a lot of graduates who know the words but do not know how to relate them to the real thing" (Jones, 1984, p. 196).

Workshops Workshops are a common method of inservice training. But for workshops to produce meaningful improvements in practice, they must possess several characteristics: active participation, opportunities for sharing among colleagues, and follow-up sessions as teachers attempt to implement the ideas (Gowen, 1987; Jones, 1986; Knox, 1977). Undertaking the Head Start Leadership Training Program, Bloom et al. (1991) noted: "One-time workshops on broad, global topics have little lasting impact on behavior. Research provides strong evidence that training is far more effective when it focuses on participants' needs, takes place over a period of time, and addresses the site-specific concerns of the individual's work setting" (p. 3).

Models and mentors Both pre- and inservice training are more effective when trainees can observe programs that demonstrate high-quality caregiving practices (Fenichel & Eggbear, 1990). Beginning teachers also benefit from having master teachers serve as role models (Greenman, 1984; Knowles, 1984). Not incidentally, the opportunity to serve as mentor for others may encourage experienced teachers to remain in the field (Whitebook et al., 1990).

Individualized supervision To implement and sustain the lessons learned in training, practitioners need ongoing one-to-one contact with a supervisor. The supervisory relationship encourages teachers and providers to reflect on their practices in a supportive atmosphere (Fenichel & Eggbear, 1990). An effective method for providing supervision is a cycle of observation, feedback, and discussion. Practitioner and supervisor collaborate to document and evaluate program practices (Rogers, Waller, & Perrin, 1987). This field-based consultation allows caregivers to think analytically about their work and to "generate theory out of practice" (Jones, 1984, p. 192). The role of advisor in the Child Development Associate (CDA) program is a good example of using field-based consultation with practitioners who lack extensive preservice training. Although formal training can be incorporated into an individualized CDA portfolio, the certification is awarded primarily on the basis of demonstrated competence rather than academic performance (Lombardi, 1989).

Work Environment

> The supply and quality of early childhood programs are being strangled by an inability to attract and retain qualified employees. This problem exists because of the inadequate compensation, low status, and poor working conditions which typify the field. Combined with an unprecedented demand for services, this constitutes a crisis for the early childhood profession and the nation (National Association for the Education of Young Children, 1984b).

The characteristics of the work environment can have a profound effect on program quality. Agency practices determine both the existence of training options and their potential impact on services to children and families. Working conditions may maximize an agency's investment in the training of caregivers, or they may negate them, as when poor working conditions lead trained teachers to leave the field. These environmental factors may be extrinsic (agency-based) or intrinsic (within the teacher), but their combined impact on teaching practices is significant (e.g., Feeney & Chun, 1985; Whitebook et al., 1989).

Extrinsic factors Organizational policy toward inservice training dictates whether and what training options are available to early childhood staff. Administrative support for ongoing training and curriculum implementation is a key determinant of program quality. Agencies manifest their support by making necessary resources, such as training facilities and program supplies, directly available to teachers (Greenman, 1984). Administrators also evidence their commitment to training in the content of their contacts with staff members. For example, program quality may be improved if administrators devote more time to program-development issues than to managerial issues during agency-wide staff meetings (Moore & Smith, 1987). In short, administrators' verbal commitments to program implementation must be backed up with the necessary time and resources from them.

The effectiveness of training is also maximized when agencies structure both formal and informal feedback mechanisms. Staff members require ongoing supervision and evaluation to help them reflect on their performance and continue developing as professionals (Jones, 1984). To appropriately credit this growing professionalism, compensation in the form of salaries and benefits must accompany staff members' training and progress in the field. Moreover, training should be viewed as a recurring part of a career path rather than as a single, isolated event (Whitebook et al., 1990).

Intrinsic factors The National Child Care Staffing Study (Whitebook et al., 1989) emphasized the multiple ways that inservice training affects the job satisfaction of caregivers. Participation in an ongoing training program contributes to a sense of professionalism. Staff members experience a renewed sense of challenge and initiative toward their work. Perhaps most significant, training conveys a sense of importance to early childhood practitioners. Learning about child development and program practices takes the role beyond "baby-sitting" and elevates it to the appropriate position of contributing to the growth and development of other human beings.

Another workplace factor affecting staff attitudes is the perceived level of peer support. Fenichel and Eggbear (1990) stress the importance of ongoing collegial support in both the preparation and the job performance of early childhood practitioners. Conversely, lack of social and professional support systems contributes to burnout and staff turnover (Whitebook, Howes, Darrah, & Friedman, 1982). Inservice training may improve relationships with co-workers by increasing the level of teamwork and collaboration (Bloom, 1988). Programs such as the High/Scope ToT model build in opportunities for intra- and interagency networking. Caregivers often cite the fact that they work in isolation, whether literally (providing services within the confines of their own homes) or figuratively (operating in a facility with only a limited number of co-teachers). Inservice training allows agencies to bring staff together for joint professional development.

A final intrinsic factor that may be affected by inservice training is the practitioner's commitment to the agency and to the early childhood field in general. If a training program is evidence of an agency's commitment to the individual, is this commitment reciprocated? To date, logic rather than empirical evidence supports the contention that commitment works both ways. Jones (1984) speculated that the absence or presence of ongoing training may explain the difference in turnover rates between agencies who otherwise share the problems that seem endemic to the field:

> Turnover of staff is a major problem in day care, and hard work and low pay may well be the primary reasons for it. But there are day care centers characterized by unusual staff stability that pay no better than centers with higher turnover and that expect their staff to work at least as hard. What they [the centers with staff stability] have achieved is high morale, an outcome of self-respect and respect by colleagues, and the sense of being an important part of a shared task that is worth doing. Training that begins by taking the individual seriously as a person offers hope of building morale. Crash training, in which one tells people what to do and tries to make them do it, simply will not work in the long run; people so-trained are not likely to stay long. [Effective] training programs offer a commitment to caregivers *over time* (p. 200).

Inservice training programs cannot reasonably be expected to address all of the workplace issues that plague the early childhood field. Policies must be changed at national and state levels, as well as at the agency level. But it is appropriate for the ToT Evaluation to question whether those factors explicitly addressed by the model's philosophy and practices are affected by an agency's choice to participate in the High/Scope training. The evaluation can ask, Does ToT sensitize administrators to the importance of ongoing training, supervision, and implementation? Does ToT promote teamwork among staff members? Does inservice training contribute to feelings of professional self-worth by linking staff with a national network directed toward improving the quality of early childhood programs?

The High/Scope Training of Trainers Projects

The High/Scope Curriculum for Young Children

Curriculum framework   The High/Scope Preschool Curriculum (Hohmann, Banet, & Weikart, 1979; Hohmann & Weikart, in press) is a coordinated set of ideas and practices based on child development principles. Its central tenet of *active learning* states that children learn best from activities that they plan and carry out themselves. Following the principles of *room arrangement*, staff arrange and label interest areas. They also maintain a *daily routine* that permits teachers and children to work together with mutual respect. As part of this routine, children choose their own activities, using a *plan-do-review process* that develops their initiative, sense of responsibility, problem-solving ability, social cooperation, and individual competence. Throughout the day, teachers build on children's existing strengths by observing and supporting children's activities in a way that promotes *key experiences* for learning.

The curriculum model is far from a scaled-down version of traditional elementary education. High/Scope emphasizes the development of language, cognitive, physical, and social skills that are developmentally appropriate to the age group being served. Implementation of the curriculum requires no special materials or equipment and can thus be adapted to a wide range of populations, geographical locations, and program settings.

Curriculum evaluation   Nearly 30 years of longitudinal research on the High/Scope Perry Preschool Project (Berrueta-Clement, Schweinhart, Barnett, Epstein, & Weikart, 1984), as well as the High/Scope Curriculum Comparison study (Schweinhart, Weikart, & Larner, 1986), indicates that the High/Scope Preschool Curriculum produces both immediate and long-term benefits to at-risk children. At age 19, youths who had attended High/Scope's Perry Preschool program compared favorably with a control group who had not participated in the program: The former preschool participants had experienced a lower rate of special education placement while in school and a higher rate of high school graduation. They also reported a lower rate of adolescent pregnancy and lower rates of delinquent and criminal acts. After high school, they were more likely to pursue postsecondary education and training, less likely to use social services and public assistance, and more likely to be employed. Economic analysis (Barnett, 1985) indicated that the costs of the Perry Preschool program were more than offset by the subsequent savings to society in decreased educational, welfare, and court expenses. As stated by the Research and Policy Council Committee on the Committee for Economic Development (1985):

> If we examine the [High/Scope] Perry Preschool Program for its investment return and convert all costs and benefits into current values based on a 3% real rate of interest, one year of the program is an extraordinary economic buy. It would be hard to imagine that society could find a higher yield for a dollar investment than that found in preschool programs for at-risk children (p. 44).

Since High/Scope's Perry Preschool and Curriculum Comparison studies in the 1960s, the percentage of the nation's 3- and 4-year-olds enrolled in early childhood programs has more than doubled (Schweinhart, 1985). The perceived value of preprimary education has resulted in a demand for high-quality programs among middle-income as well as low-income groups, and among a variety of other at-risk populations, including children with special needs, young children of teenaged parents, and children from multilingual families. Those implementing or considering implementing the High/Scope Curriculum today wonder if it can demonstrate an impact on the lives of children attending these programs in the 1980s and 1990s. Can the findings of High/Scope's earlier evaluations, based on relatively small samples within a limited geographic area, be replicated with larger numbers of children living in a diversity of environments throughout the country today? That question about the curriculum's present-day validity is an important component of this ToT Evaluation.

High/Scope's Training History

The success of the High/Scope Perry Preschool program was surely dependent on the high quality of the educational services delivered to the children and their families. The research we cited earlier substantiates that one mechanism for improving and maintaining program quality is intensive inservice staff training. From 1981 to 1991, in response to the rapid growth of early childhood programs, the High/Scope Foundation's consultants conducted training projects for teachers and early childhood caregivers in 45 states, the District of Columbia, Puerto Rico, the Virgin Islands, and 19 countries abroad. This training occurred on site; at the High/Scope Foundation headquarters in Ypsilanti, Michigan; and at centralized locations in diverse geographical areas. Table 1 lists all the locations in the United States and abroad where High/Scope, as of 1991, had conducted Training of Trainers and other inservice training projects.

Given the large numbers of teachers who might benefit from training, however, High/Scope came to realize early on that if training was to include continued follow-up and monitoring of program quality, direct training of *teaching staff* was neither cost-effective nor feasible. Moreover, direct training did not take advantage of the many early childhood specialists and supervisors, already on agency staffs, who were in a unique position to train and monitor those working in the local centers and day care homes of their agencies. Consequently, beginning in 1981 we designed and began implementing the High/Scope Training of Trainers (ToT) projects to train key personnel, who would in turn train large numbers of teachers and caregivers in their sponsoring agencies.

The first ToT project was implemented in 1981–82, when the Los Angeles County Head Start/State Preschool System contracted with High/Scope to begin a series of training workshops. High/Scope also trained staff in Missouri during that year, and 3 years later, in 1984–85, launched projects in Fairfax, Virginia, and Riverside, California. Also in 1984–85 the Foundation launched its first international venture in Great Britain with the cooperation of the Voluntary Organisations Liaison Council for Under Fives (VOLCUF). In the decade from 1981 to 1991 High/Scope conducted 80 ToT projects with trainees from 38 states and 12 foreign countries. Of the 1,500 project participants, 1,075 have become endorsed High/Scope trainers. The

Table 1

COMPLETED, ONGOING, AND SCHEDULED HIGH/SCOPE TRAINING IN
THE UNITED STATES AND ABROAD AS OF 1991

Location	No. of ToT Projects	Number of Other Training Projects[a]
United States		
Alabama	—	2
Arizona	1	10
Arkansas	1	—
California	20	26
Colorado	2	4
Connecticut	—	4
District of Columbia	—	2
Florida	2	37
Georgia	2	9
Hawaii	—	1
Iowa	—	5
Idaho	—	5
Illinois	4	27
Indiana	—	5
Kansas	—	8
Kentucky	—	8
Louisiana	—	2
Maine	—	2
Maryland	—	2
Massachusetts	1	8
Michigan	14	25
Minnesota	—	25
Mississippi	1	3
Missouri	1	12
Nebraska	1	14
Nevada	—	1
New Hampshire	—	1
New Jersey	2	4
New Mexico	—	3
New York	8	38
North Carolina	—	8
Ohio	1	21
Oklahoma	1	1
Oregon	1	7
Pennsylvania	1	26
Puerto Rico	3	1

Table 1 (continued)

COMPLETED, ONGOING, AND SCHEDULED HIGH/SCOPE TRAINING IN THE UNITED STATES AND ABROAD AS OF 1991

Location	No. of ToT Projects	Number of Other Training Projects[a]
Rhode Island	—	1
South Carolina	2	2
Tennessee	—	8
Texas	2	20
Utah	—	2
Vermont	—	5
Virginia	2	22
Virgin Islands	—	1
Washington	1	12
West Virginia	—	2
Wisconsin	1	25
Wyoming	—	4
U.S. subtotal	75	461
Other Countries		
Australia	—	1
Brazil	—	1
Canada	—	16
Chile	—	1
Columbia	—	1
Denmark	—	1
Germany	—	2
Israel	—	1
Korea	—	1
Mexico	—	1
Netherlands	—	1
New Zealand	—	1
Norway	1	1
Peru	—	1
Portugal	—	1
South Africa	1	1
Turkey	—	1
United Kingdom	3	1
Venezuela	—	1
Foreign subtotal	5	35
World total	80	496

[a]Includes curriculum and training workshops in infancy, early childhood, K–3, adolescence, and music and movement

High/Scope Registry survey (reported in Chapter 4) documented that the High/Scope endorsed trainers on average had worked with 25 agency staff, which typically meant a dozen teaching teams. Thus ToT, within its first decade, was able to disseminate the High/Scope training and curriculum model to an estimated 25,000 early childhood practitioners serving 250,000 children annually throughout the country.

Funding for the ToT projects has come from a variety of public and private sources. Public sources have included training money from Head Start agencies, state and municipal education funds, and departments of social services. Major private contributors have been the Ford Foundation, for training throughout the country; W. K. Kellogg Foundation, for training in Michigan; and the Aaron Diamond Foundation, for ToT projects in the New York City metropolitan area. Numerous regional and local organizations have also contributed to training activities in their areas. Investment in ToT is viewed by all these supporters as an effective mechanism for enhancing local-agency capability and maintaining program quality and consistency over a sustained period.

The Training of Trainers Model

Purpose The ToT projects prepare early childhood specialists and supervisors to train classroom teachers and other caregivers in implementing the High/Scope Preschool Curriculum. Prospective trainers are drawn from a wide variety of early childhood agencies, public schools, and colleges. Their training covers in depth the Foundation's developmentally valid curriculum, an educational approach that emphasizes children's active learning in a supportive environment structured by adults. Training participants also learn appropriate strategies for conducting inservice training with the practitioners in their agencies. Training of Trainers prepares them to work with classroom teachers and aides, day care providers in homes and centers, agency administrators, and parents of children in their programs.

Content Each ToT project provides 20 to 25 participants with 35 days of on-site training, conducted in seven 5-day sessions over 10 to 12 months. Participants are assessed according to their performance in training activities that include workshops, seminars, reading and reflective-writing tasks, classroom observation and feedback, and individual consultations. Each training project includes the following activities:

- *Workshop and seminar sessions.* All participants meet with the High/Scope consultant at a location central to them (for training and curriculum workshops) and at their programs (for classroom observation and feedback sessions). Workshops and seminars focus on adult learning and training strategies and on developmentally appropriate practices for children.

- *Training assignments.* In the weeks between training sessions, participants adapt and apply at their own agencies what they are learning about working with staff to implement the High/Scope Curriculum. Participants train teaching teams, observe and give feedback to staff, develop a training classroom, present workshops to staff and parents, meet with administrators, assess program implementation and child growth, document their training activities, and record their reflections in project journals.

- *Feedback and evaluation.* The High/Scope consultant provides training participants with verbal and written feedback on their assignments. Participants are evaluated on their workshop presentations, observation and feedback techniques, level of curriculum implementation in the training classroom, and overall participation in the project.

Quality assurance   Going beyond the basic licensing requirements, the ToT inservice training model is designed to incorporate key components of quality in early childhood programs. Model design assures the following:

- *A valid developmental curriculum* that serves as a decision-making framework and ensures coherent and purposeful behavior by teachers and caregivers in response to the needs of individual children

- *Staff training* in the curriculum, and supervision through an ongoing training and monitoring system

- *Staff support* from colleagues and administrators, who work in teams to plan and implement the program

- *Parent involvement* in classroom and home activities; recognition of parents as the primary educators of their own children; linkage of parents with support services in the community, as necessary

- *Continuous evaluation* of teaching practices and children's progress, as a mechanism for monitoring program quality and ensuring continued program development

A more detailed description of the training methods and the course content of the High/Scope Training of Trainers model follows in Chapter 2.

Evaluation Overview

The ToT Evaluation examined the diffusion of the Foundation's training and curriculum model as it passed from High/Scope consultant to trainer to teacher to child. To provide a comprehensive look at these interlocking steps, the evaluation design called for three related studies of trainers, teachers, and children. Each of these studies is briefly described in the remainder of this chapter and summarized in Table 2. Details about the study methodology and results are reported in the chapters devoted to each of these evaluation components.

Table 2

DESIGN OF THE HIGH/SCOPE TRAINING OF TRAINERS (ToT) EVALUATION
(1989–1992)

Chain of Transmission	Evaluation Component	Sample	Measurement Technique(s)	Issues Addressed
High/Scope consultant to trainer	*Trainer Study*	*793 ToT candidates* (from 40 projects, national sample)	*Process analysis* ■ Consultant debriefings ■ Candidate journals ■ Candidate evaluations ■ Ethnographer observations	■ Reflections on ToT participation ■ Curriculum & training insights ■ On-site training ■ Parent reactions to the curriculum ■ Child reactions to the curriculum
		203 endorsed trainers (national sample)	*Registry survey*	■ Agency affiliation ■ Education & experience ■ Job title & roles ■ Training activities: amount & type ■ Level of implementation
Trainer to teacher	*Teacher Study*	*366 teachers* (244 High/Scope, 122 comparison; in NY, CA, MI)	*Teacher telephone interviews*	■ Agency/job description ■ Inservice training ■ Background information ■ Organizational climate
			Program observations ■ Program Implementation Profile ■ Early Childhood Environment Rating Scale ■ Arnett Global Rating Scale	■ Physical environment ■ Program routine ■ Adult-child interaction ■ Opportunities for learning: cognitive, social, emotional, language, creativity, motor, multicultural ■ Teacher style & sensitivity
Teacher to child	*Child Study*	*200 children* (97 High/Scope, 103 comparison; aged 2–6; in MI only)	*Child Observation Record*	■ Initiative ■ Social relations ■ Creative representation ■ Language & literacy ■ Logic & mathematics ■ Music & movement
			DIAL-R	■ Standardized measure: motor area, concepts area, language area

The Trainer Study

The Trainer Study documented attitudes and activities of participants during and after High/Scope ToT projects. This component was made up of two parts. The *process analysis* used anecdotal records to provide insights into the experience of attending ToT sessions and practicing the skills covered in the workshops. The *Registry survey* examined the subsequent activities of endorsed trainers, to document the extent to which training continued to take place at their sponsoring agencies.

1. The process analysis

Sample. Insights into the ToT process were based on anecdotal records of the High/Scope consultants and 793 candidates in 40 training projects completed between 1987 and 1991. These projects were geographically diverse and comprised a wide variety of urban and rural locations and early childhood program settings.

Research procedures. The author of this report prepared individual final reports for the 40 ToT projects and then conducted a cross-project content analysis of their findings. The primary purpose of these reports was to identify issues—both positive and negative—that emerged during the training project. Insights were derived from three sources of information: debriefing forms completed by the project consultants, journals completed by a sample of candidates in each project, and final evaluation forms completed by all the candidates in the 40 projects. In one of the projects, additional data were provided by a second member of the research staff, who acted as an ethnographer by sitting in on training sessions and observing candidates at their practice sites.

Areas addressed. Cross-project analyses and ethnographic observations provided a comprehensive view of ToT projects from the perspective of the participants. The issues raised were synthesized to examine five areas:

- Reflections on participating in the ToT sessions and activities

- Content insights regarding the curriculum and training techniques

- On-site experiences conducting training with staff members

- Parent reactions to the curriculum

- Child reactions to the curriculum

2. The High/Scope Registry survey

Sample. A national sample of 203 trainers was randomly selected from the *High/Scope Registry 1989 Directory* (a complete listing of all those who by March 1989 had been endorsed to conduct training in the High/Scope Curriculum). Respondents came from all areas of the country and represented a variety of early childhood settings: Head Start, public school, and both nonprofit and for-profit agencies. All the trainers had participated in ToT projects within the past 7 years, with 32 months the average elapsed time since completion.

Research procedures. A member of the High/Scope evaluation team used a questionnaire to conduct an individual telephone survey with each of the endorsed trainers.

Areas addressed. High/Scope endorsed trainers provided the following information:

- Agency affiliation

- Education and job experience

- Job title and responsibilities

- Training activities (amount and type)

- Degree of High/Scope Curriculum implementation by teachers

The Registry survey was conducted and originally reported by Larner and Schweinhart (1991).

The Teacher Study

The Teacher Study looked at inservice training and its relationship to teaching practices. It assessed the extent to which the High/Scope Curriculum was actually being implemented in classrooms and compared program quality in High/Scope and non-High/Scope (comparison) sites. This study had two components: First, *teacher telephone interviews* examined support for training and implementation from the perspective of High/Scope and comparison teachers. Second, *program observations* looked at the actual teaching practices in High/Scope and comparison programs.

1. The teacher telephone interviews

Sample. A sample of 366 early childhood programs was identified in Michigan, California, and New York. Of the total sample, 244 (67 percent) were High/Scope programs, and 122 (33 percent) were comparison programs. They represented the same range of early childhood agencies as did those subjects in the Registry survey. The lead teachers from the 366 programs made up the interview sample.

Research procedures. Trained interviewers from Michigan used the High/Scope Teacher Telephone Interview to conduct all telephone interviews. Interviewers did not know whether teachers were from the High/Scope or the comparison group.

Areas addressed. Interviewed teachers answered a variety of questions concerning training and program implementation in their agencies. They supplied information about

- Their agencies and job descriptions

- Inservice training offered by their agencies (amount, type, and content)

- Their background characteristics (education, experience)

- The organizational climate in their agencies

2. Program implementation observations

Sample. The same sample of 366 early childhood programs made up the observation sample. In actuality, so items discussed during the interviews would not influence teaching practices, the program observations preceded the teacher interviews. Also, in each case, the research staff member conducting the observation was different from the staff member conducting the teacher interview.

Research procedures. Programs were assessed using three observational measures: the Arnett Global Rating Scale (adapted from a measure used in the National Child Care Staffing Study; Arnett, 1989); the Early Childhood Environment Rating Scale (ECERS; Harms & Clifford, 1980); and a generic adaptation of the Program Implementation Profile (PIP; High/Scope Educational Research Foundation, 1989). The observations were conducted by trained observers who were recruited from each of the three geographical locations and brought to High/Scope for training. Like the teacher interviewers, the program observers did not know whether subjects (programs) belonged to the High/Scope or the comparison group.

Areas addressed. The use of three distinct observational instruments allowed researchers to look at a wide range of program practices and teacher characteristics. Among the issues examined were these:

- Physical environment

- Program routine

- Adult-child interaction

- Opportunities for learning in all areas of development

- Teacher style and sensitivity

The Child Study

The Child Study looked at the last link in the chain—the effect of various program practices on children's development. Observations provided an in-depth look at children in High/Scope programs. In addition, the study allowed the Foundation to conduct an up-to-date comparison of the effects of High/Scope versus other curriculum models.

Sample. To permit the collection of detailed information within time and budget limitations, the sample of 200 children was drawn entirely from Michigan. Of the total sample, 97 (48.5 percent) were from High/Scope programs and 103 (51.5 percent) were from comparison sites. Although the sample was restricted to one state, care was taken to include children from a range of agencies and populations that was similar to the range sampled in the total program group.

Research procedures. Children were assessed with two measures: the High/Scope Child Observation Record (COR) for Ages 2½–6 (High/Scope Educational Research Foundation, 1992), which is a generic adaptation of an instrument originally designed to document children's progress in High/Scope programs; and the DIAL-R (Mardell-Czudnowski & Goldenberg, 1990), which is a widely used screening test of children's abilities. [*Note:* Readers

22

may obtain copies of instruments used in the ToT Evaluation from the following sources: the instrument's publisher (ECERS and DIAL-R); the instrument's developer (Arnett); or the High/Scope Foundation (all other instruments).]

Areas addressed. The observation measure looked at children's development in six areas:

- Initiative

- Social relations

- Creative representation

- Language and literacy

- Logic and mathematical relations

- Music and movement

The screening test examined children's abilities in three domains:

- Motor area

- Concepts area

- Language area

Organization of the Evaluation Report

The remainder of this report explores the procedures and results of the ToT Evaluation and examines their implications for improving early childhood programs through systematic inservice training. Chapter 2 explains the process and content of High/Scope ToT projects in detail—the training model for adults and the curriculum model for young children. Chapters 3 and 4 cover the two components of the Trainer Study—the *process analysis* with ToT participants and the *Registry survey* with endorsed trainers. Chapters 5 and 6 report on the two parts of the Teacher Study—the *teacher interviews* and the *program observations* with both High/Scope and comparison programs. Chapter 7 is devoted to the Child Study of curriculum effects and of the relationship of training and program quality to child measures. Finally, Chapter 8 integrates the findings from all the evaluation components and discusses their policy implications in light of the training and curriculum issues raised in this chapter.

II The High/Scope Training and Curriculum Models

High/Scope provides both a training model for adults and a curriculum model for young children. In a High/Scope Training of Trainers (ToT) project, groups of 20 to 25 adults (trainer candidates) meet with a High/Scope consultant in a year-long series of workshops and practice activities. These candidates learn how to present hands-on workshops to their staff, and they train teachers in one or more "training classrooms" to implement the High/Scope Curriculum. At the end of the project, candidates who have successfully completed all the training requirements are certified as High/Scope endorsed trainers, qualified to train others in the implementation of the High/Scope Preschool Curriculum. In the High/Scope Curriculum, children are engaged in a developmental process of active learning. Rooms are arranged to facilitate children's independence and easy access to diverse materials. Children make plans, carry out activities of their own choice, and review what they have done. Teachers play an active role in supporting children's learning by observing their interests, asking open-ended questions, and setting up problem-solving situations. Adults and children together create opportunities for the key experiences that promote learning.

The High/Scope approach to early childhood programs has two distinctive components. One is the training model for adults, and the other is the curriculum model for young children. In this chapter, we describe the underlying framework and content of the High/Scope Training of Trainers (ToT) course and the High/Scope Preschool Curriculum. The Trainer and Teacher Studies reported in subsequent chapters (3–6) evaluated the effectiveness of the High/Scope dissemination model for adults. The Child Study (Chapter 7) examined the merits of the High/Scope Curriculum relative to other programs.

The High/Scope Training of Trainers Model for Adults

Rationale

The High/Scope Training of Trainers (ToT) program prepares early childhood specialists and curriculum supervisors to train adults working with young children in the High/Scope Curriculum. The program's dual focus on a preschool curriculum method and adult-training strategies is intended to make participants knowledgeable about appropriate program practices and skillful at bringing about program change. ToT is designed as a cost-effective approach for preparing *trainers* to work with early childhood practitioners. In place of the recurring costs of contracting with a succession of outside consultants, agencies can acquire an in-house training resource with a single investment in ToT. Developing this local, on-site training capability is not only cost-effective, it is also learning-effective. An agency-based trainer can establish an ongoing relationship with teaching staff, provide coherent and consistent training, and insure adequate follow-up to sustain program improvements.

Training Approach

Each ToT project serves 20 to 25 candidates drawn from a variety of early childhood agencies within a given geographical target area (metropolitan, state, or regional). High/Scope works with local, state, and regional organizations within the target area to recruit a sufficient number of interested agencies who will commit to participation in a ToT project. The Foundation also assists groups in obtaining funding from private and public sources to cover the costs of the training.

High/Scope meets with agency administrators to explain the project requirements and to insure that appropriate persons are selected for project participation. Administrators are encouraged to select candidates with a solid background in early childhood education and with demonstrated ability to do training. They select, for example, curriculum supervisors, educational specialists, lead teachers, and day care directors. Candidates who successfully complete all the ToT course requirements are then certified as endorsed High/Scope trainers (see Endorsement Requirements on page 29).

ToT candidates are actively involved in a 1-year inservice training program that includes the following components:

- *Thirty-five days of workshop sessions.* All participants and the High/ Scope consultant meet in a central location for curriculum and training workshops and for observation-and-feedback sessions. Typically the workshops are conducted as seven week-long sessions spread over 10 to 12 months.

- *Training assignments.* Participants complete reading and writing tasks and are actively involved in group work during the training project. In the weeks between workshops, participants return to their agencies to apply knowledge acquired at the workshop. They train teaching teams, observe and give feedback to teachers, conduct workshops, meet with support staff, and document this training process in written assignments and journals.

- *Feedback and evaluation.* High/Scope consultants give periodic feedback to ToT participants on the assignments they have completed during the training project. They also periodically visit each training site to assess candidates' skills in the areas of workshop presentations, teacher observation and feedback, and curriculum implementation in the training classroom.

Course Content

The ToT program covers a series of curriculum and training topics. The order of presentation and the length of time spent on each topic varies slightly from project to project, depending on the composition of the group and the consultant's assessment of their skills. Related topics may be added to the syllabus, based on candidates' needs and interests. (See pages 27 and 28 for a sample 7-week workshop sequence.)

Sample Training of Trainers (ToT) 7-Week Workshop Sequence

Week 1

Monday

- Introduction to the training project
- Research and the elements of quality

Tuesday

- How children learn
- Active learning

Wednesday

- Classroom observation
- Observation-related discussion

Thursday

- Arranging the learning environment
- Classroom materials and equipment

Friday

- Role of the trainer (administrators attend)
- Training plans and individual meetings

Week 2

Monday

- Issues review
- Introduction to the daily routine

Tuesday

- Plan-do-review (full-day session)

Wednesday

- Adult learning
- How to present workshops

Thursday

- Curriculum review
- Using the *Program Implementation Profile (PIP)*

Friday

- The change process
- Training plans and individual meetings

Week 3

Monday

- Issues/review
- Adult-child interaction

Tuesday

- Small-group time (full-day session)

Wednesday

- Key experiences (full-day session)

Thursday

- Key experiences (continued)
- Collaboration

Friday

- Collaboration (continued)
- Training plans and individual meetings

Week 4

Monday

- Issues/review
- Lesson planning and the *Child Observation Record (COR)*

Tuesday

- K–3 implementation
- Special education implementation

Wednesday

- Observation and feedback
- How to present workshops

(Continued on p. 28)

Sample Training Sequence *(continued)*

Thursday

- Workshop planning and individual assessment (full-day session)

Friday

- Workshop planning and individual assessment (full-day session)

Week 5

Monday

- Issues/review
- Social/emotional development

Tuesday

- Peer workshop: Representation
- Child management

Wednesday

- Peer workshop: Language development
- Supporting diversity and multicultural education

Thursday

- Peer workshop: Classification
- Peer workshop: Seriation

Friday

- Peer workshop: Number
- Training plans and individual meetings

Week 6

Monday

- Issues/review
- Child-assessment exercise

Tuesday

- Teaching and feedback (full-day session)

Wednesday

- Teaching and feedback (full-day session)

Thursday

- Peer workshop: Spatial relations
- Music and movement

Friday

- Peer workshop: Helping children make choices
- Training plans and individual meetings

Week 7

Monday

- Issues/review
- Parent involvement

Tuesday

- Peer workshop: Time
- Literacy

Wednesday

- Peer workshop: Play in the block area
- Implementation with infants and toddlers

Thursday

- Peer workshop: Outdoor play spaces
- Key experiences review

Friday

- Final evaluation, networking

Endorsement Requirements

ToT is a graduate-level program leading to certification as a High/Scope endorsed trainer for those who successfully complete all seven of the following requirements:

1. Establishing a classroom that implements the High/Scope Curriculum model

2. Planning and conducting training workshops

3. Observing program implementation and giving feedback to staff

4. Completing on-site training plans and assignments

5. Writing a reflective journal during the training program

6. Developing lesson plans based on the methods of the curriculum

7. Participating in a team and attending all training sessions

Using a standard grading system developed for each of the seven requirements, the High/Scope consultant conducting the training evaluates each candidate. At the end of the project, each participant receives a High/Scope transcript categorizing the training into three courses: How Children Learn, How Adults Learn, and High/Scope Curriculum Implementation. To achieve endorsement, a candidate must have a grade point average of 3.0 or better in each of these three courses.

The High/Scope Registry

Candidates who successfully complete the endorsement requirements become members of the International High/Scope Registry. The Registry is a professional organization designed to

- Promote standards of quality for those who teach preschool-aged and school-aged children according to High/Scope-approved curricula

- Promote standards of quality for persons who train and supervise educators in High/Scope programs

- Promote standards of quality for individual programs adopting the High/Scope approach

- Promote communication and information-sharing among early childhood professionals through newsletters, conferences, and association activities

- Promote the continued development and refinement of the body of knowledge and skills that are the foundation of the developmentally appropriate High/Scope curricula

- Provide and facilitate continuing professional education opportunities for Registry members and for persons interested in becoming Registry members

The High/Scope Curriculum for Young Children

Overview

The High/Scope Preschool Curriculum is a coordinated set of ideas and practices in early childhood education first formulated in the 1960s and 1970s by the staff of the High/Scope Educational Research Foundation, under the leadership of David P. Weikart. The curriculum is comprehensively described in the High/Scope Press publication *Young Children in Action: A Manual for Preschool Educators* (Hohmann, Banet, & Weikart, 1979; Hohmann & Weikart, in press). In the 1980s, the Foundation integrated several innovations into the basic curriculum model, including the use of computers and adaptations for special needs children and for populations in programs being implemented overseas.

The High/Scope Curriculum is based on Jean Piaget's constructivist theories of child development. The curriculum rests on the fundamental premise that children are active learners, who learn best from activities that they themselves plan, carry out, and reflect on. In the High/Scope Curriculum, teachers and children work together in an atmosphere of mutual respect. No special materials are required; the classroom is equipped, like any good nursery school, with a variety of easily accessible manipulative materials. Teachers arrange interest areas in the classroom and maintain a daily routine that permits children to plan, carry out, and review activities of their own choosing. During these activities, teachers join in the children's play and ask questions to extend their thinking skills. Teachers encourage various key experiences that help children develop basic cognitive and socioemotional processes, such as placing things in order, predicting consequences, collaborating with peers, and describing and sharing activities with others.

Active Learning by the Child

The critical principle of the High/Scope Curriculum is that teachers must be fully committed to providing settings in which children learn actively and construct their own knowledge. The child's knowledge comes from personal interaction with the world, from direct experience with real objects, and from reflection and the application of logical thinking to this experience. The impetus to learn comes from within the child. Children's interests and intentions lead them to explore, experiment, question, and construct new knowledge and understanding. This active learning approach is in contrast to didactic model approaches, in which adults determine the content of instruction and then teach it to the child in a rote-drill or directive manner. It also differs from the traditional nursery school approach, in which the exploration of certain themes, such as holidays or seasons, is programmed by the teacher, and the child is otherwise involved in free-choice play.

The High/Scope Curriculum identifies five ingredients of active learning for young children:

1. **Materials** for the child to explore
2. **Manipulation** of materials by the child
3. **Choices** by the child about what to do with the materials
4. **Language** from the child
5. **Support** from the adult

Room Arrangement

The physical environment is the setting for active learning. In the High/Scope Curriculum, classrooms are divided into areas, such as house, art, block, and quiet areas. Low dividers and shelves, which make it possible for children to see all parts of the room, define the various areas and at the same time provide storage space for diverse materials. The supplies in each area are easily accessible to the children and numerous enough so several children can use the same materials simultaneously. Areas and the materials in them are labeled with a variety of symbols, including drawings, photographs, words, and actual objects. This system helps children develop logical representations of their environment. Easy access to supplies and the orderly arrangement of the room also promote independence, since children can find and put away materials on their own.

The Daily Routine

Another important part of the framework for active learning is the daily routine. Just as room arrangement physically defines children's activities (determining where and with what materials they play), the daily routine temporally defines their activities. It determines how children use the physical environment and interact with peers and adults *over time*. The consistency of the daily routine allows children to have a sense of control over their environment, to predict when and how things will happen, and to feel comfortable in exercising their independence.

The heart of the High/Scope daily routine is the **plan-do-review** process, whereby children make choices about what they will do, carry out their own ideas, and reflect on their activities. In addition to this plan-do-review sequence, the High/Scope Curriculum builds **small-** and **large-group** activities into the daily routine. The elements of the daily routine are these:

Planning time Children make choices and decisions all the time, but seldom do we encourage them to think about actions or their consequences in a systematic way. Planning time gives children a structured and consistent opportunity to express their ideas to adults and peers and to see themselves as acting on their own decisions. In this first step of the daily routine, children individually talk over their plans with a teacher. To get an understanding of the child's developmental level and encourage elaboration of the plan, the teacher may ask questions or respond to the child's suggestions. This process helps children to form a mental picture of their ideas and of the materials they will need to carry them out.

Work time   Work time is the "do" part of the plan-do-review sequence, the period that follows planning. Generally the longest single segment in the daily routine, it is a busy period for both children and adults. As children execute their plans, adults are actively observing and entering into children's play. Adults ask questions, set up problem-solving situations, refer children to one another for help, and develop ideas for materials and activities that may extend children's learning in the days and weeks ahead.

Cleanup time   At the end of work time comes cleanup time. As noted earlier, the orderly arrangement and labeling of the room permit children to play an active and independent role in putting away the materials they have used during work time. At the same time that they learn such skills as classification and seriation, children develop a sense of pride in their self-sufficiency.

Recall time   Recall time is the final phase of the plan-do-review sequence. The children represent their work in a variety of developmentally appropriate ways, using words, actions, and visual representations. They might recall the names of the children who helped them carry out their plan, draw a picture of the building they made, or act out for teachers and peers how they solved a problem they encountered. Recall time brings closure to planning and work time activities. With questions and comments, teachers help children make the linkage between their original plan and the work they accomplished.

Snack time   Snacks are more than an opportunity to provide children with nutritious food. Eating together is a social occasion in which children and adults may continue to reflect on the day's events and anticipate the activities to come. Serving and eating the food also provide many opportunities for children to experience and discuss the physical and sensory characteristics of the items at the table. For example, in helping to distribute the snacks, children learn about one-to-one correspondence; while tasting the food, they may also comment on color, size, shape, or number.

Small-group time   The format of small-group time is similar in all early childhood programs: The teacher presents an activity in which children participate for a set period of time. Activities may be drawn from the cultural background of the children, from field trips the group has taken, from the seasons of the year, or from age-appropriate group projects involving cooking, art, music, and so on. Small-group time in the High/Scope Curriculum is distinguished by several factors. Although the teacher initially structures the activity, children are encouraged to contribute their own ideas and to solve problems in their own way. There is no prescribed sequence and no specified product for children to make. There are ample materials, so group members can work simultaneously without waiting for access to basic supplies. As children work with the materials, teachers extend their activities by asking open-ended questions, setting up additional problems, and encouraging children to observe one another and share with others what they are doing.

Large-group, circle time   At circle time, the whole group meets together with an adult for 10 to 15 minutes to play games, sing songs, do finger-plays, do basic movement exercises, or reenact a special event. Circle time provides an opportunity for each child to participate in a large-group situation, share and demonstrate ideas, and imitate and expand on the ideas of others.

Outside time   Outside time is a chance for children to exercise large muscles. However, the focus is not limited to motor development but is an extension of all facets of development to the outdoor setting. Children can plan, carry out, and evaluate their outdoor as well as their indoor activities. Playground equipment not only encourages jumping and climbing but also becomes a physical structure for engaging in dramatic play. The outdoor setting allows children to observe differences in temperature, sound, smell, and space. Adults support children during outside time in the same way they do at work time—by entering into play, asking open-ended questions, and extending activities.

Key Experiences

Children's interactions with the world can be characterized by a set of key experiences that help them encounter and understand their environment. While plan-do-review is the central daily concern of the child, key experiences are the central themes that help teachers think about the day. Key experiences are the conceptual framework that teachers use to make sure that children learn and develop appropriately during their chosen activities. We use the word *key* because the experiences are essential to the healthy physical, intellectual, social, and emotional growth of the young child. The next two pages list the High/Scope preschool key experiences in 10 different areas of learning.

The Role of the Adult

Teachers as well as children are active learners in the High/Scope Curriculum. By observing children's activities, teachers achieve new insights into each child's unique skills and interests. Through daily evaluation and team planning, teachers use these insights to create a challenging environment and to support children's learning. The role of observation is crucial to this process. To guide their observations of children, teachers use the High/Scope Child Observation Record (COR), an assessment tool with rating scales based on the key experiences.[5]

Throughout the daily routine, adults function in a supportive and guiding role. Teachers listen closely to what children plan, observe what

---

[5]The ToT participants who took part in the Training of Trainers Evaluation were trained to use earlier versions of the Child Observation Record (COR) and to make daily anecdotal notes using a form called the Child Assessment Record (CAR). The current version of the COR, used in the Child Study and described in Chapter 7, supplies teachers with Anecdotal Notecards to record their daily observations.

The High/Scope Preschool Key Experiences

Creative Representation

- Recognizing objects by sight, sound, touch, taste, and smell
- Imitating actions and sounds
- Relating pictures, photographs, and models to real places and things
- Pretending and role-playing
- Making models out of clay, blocks, etc.
- Drawing and painting

Language and Literacy

- Talking with others about personally meaningful experiences
- Describing objects, events, and relations
- Having fun with language: listening to stories and poems, making up stories and rhymes
- Writing in various ways: drawing, scribbling, letter-like forms, invented spelling, conventional forms
- Reading in various ways: reading storybooks, signs, symbols, and other print materials
- Dictating stories

Social Relations/Initiative

- Making and expressing choices, plans, and decisions
- Solving problems encountered in play
- Taking care of one's own needs
- Expressing feelings in words
- Participating in group routines
- Being sensitive to the feelings, interests, and needs of others
- Building relationships with children and adults
- Creating and experiencing collaborative play
- Dealing with social conflict in constructive ways

Movement

- Moving in place
- Moving from place to place
- Moving with objects
- Describing movement
- Interpreting movement directions
- Expressing creativity in movement
- Feeling and expressing beat
- Moving with others to a common beat

Music

- Responding to music
- Making and describing sounds
- Playing simple musical instruments
- Singing

Classification

- Exploring and describing similarities, differences, and the attributes of things
- Sorting and matching
- Using and describing something in several different ways
- Distinguishing between *some* and *all*
- Holding more than one attribute in mind at a time
- Describing characteristics something does not possess or what class it does not belong to

Seriation

- Comparing attributes: longer/shorter; rougher/smoother, etc.
- Arranging several things one after another in a series or pattern and describing the relationships: big, bigger, biggest
- Fitting one ordered set of objects to another through trial and error

Number

- Comparing number and amount to determine *more, less, fewer, same amount*
- Arranging two sets of objects in one-to-one correspondence
- Counting objects, as well as counting by rote

Space

- Filling and emptying
- Fitting things together and taking them apart
- Changing the shape and arrangement of objects (folding, twisting, stretching, stacking)
- Observing things and places from different spatial viewpoints
- Experiencing and describing relative positions, directions, and distances of things in the immediate environment (play space, building, neighborhood)
- Interpreting spatial relations in drawings, pictures, and photographs

Time

- Starting and stopping an action on signal
- Experiencing and describing different rates of movement
- Experiencing and comparing time intervals
- Experiencing and anticipating change and sequences of events

they do at work time, and attend to what children remember as being significant at recall time. Through the use of open-ended questions, they expand children's thinking and extend children's activities in accordance with their interests and developmental abilities. Teachers are not limited by a defined set of facts they must impart to children. Instead, they can create a wide range of learning opportunities that permit a variety of key experiences to occur. This approach, which permits teacher and child to interact as equals in the educational process, is the antithesis of approaches involving the directive, active teacher and the passive pupil. In the High/Scope Curriculum, learning is a joint activity shared by children and adults.

The remainder of this report examines the effectiveness of the High/Scope training and curriculum models described in this chapter. To evaluate training, we looked at what candidates gained from their ToT experience and what kinds of knowledge and skills they were able to transfer to teachers at their early childhood agencies. We compared the quality of programs implemented in High/Scope settings with those offered at non-High/Scope, comparison settings. To evaluate the curriculum, we looked at the development of children attending High/Scope and comparison programs. We asked whether the High/Scope Curriculum did a better job of promoting the social, emotional, cognitive, and physical development of the young child than did other early childhood program approaches.

III The Process Analysis

The process analysis was the first piece of the two-part Trainer Study. Anecdotal records from the consultants and 793 candidates in 40 training projects were analyzed to explore the attitudes and activities of ToT participants. Candidates reported that ToT nurtured their professional growth by integrating developmental theory with practice and by introducing them to a valuable network of colleagues in early childhood education. Candidates successfully overcame teachers' resistance to change and brought about improvements in program quality and staff teamwork. They reported that parents of children in High/Scope programs increasingly respected the role of play in children's learning. And candidates stated that the curriculum helped children to become more independent, less disruptive, more verbal, more focused, and more creative.

Purpose

The Trainer Study looked at the first link in the dissemination chain of the ToT model, the transmission from consultant to trainer. This evaluation component focused on High/Scope-prepared trainers, documenting who they were, what they learned and experienced during ToT projects, and what kinds of training they subsequently conducted for their sponsoring agencies. To accomplish this end, two types of research were conducted. The first was a *process analysis* based on a content analysis of anecdotal records kept by the High/Scope consultants and 793 participants in 40 ToT projects around the country. The second was a *Registry survey*, in which a national random sample of 203 High/Scope endorsed trainers reported on their inservice training activities at High/Scope sites. The process analysis is reported in this chapter; the Registry survey is the subject of the following chapter.

The process analysis captured an insider's perspective of ToT. Evaluators looked at what candidates learned, how they learned it, and how they felt about the learning process. Information from High/Scope consultants and candidates in 40 ToT sites was synthesized to provide insights regarding the training experience. Five areas were examined: candidates' general responses to the training project, candidates' self-reported understanding of the course content, candidates' experiences with staff training, candidates' reports of parent reactions to the High/Scope Curriculum, and changes in children's behavior that candidates attributed to the High/Scope Curriculum.

Procedures

The Sample

The sample for the process analysis contained the High/Scope consultants and 793 candidates in 40 ToT projects completed between 1987 and 1991.

Table 3 lists the locations, dates, number of candidates, and number of endorsements for each of these projects. The 40 projects were geographically diverse, comprising a wide variety of urban and rural settings. Agencies represented in the projects were similarly varied, with participants from Head Start, public school, nonprofit, and for-profit early childhood settings.

Instrumentation and Data Collection

The author of this report obtained qualitative data from three sources for each of the 40 ToT projects reviewed:

- *Participant journals.* The evaluator read a total of 157 journals (approximately 4 per project) kept by candidates during their training and submitted to the evaluator by the project consultants. These journals were chronological entries in which candidates reported and reflected on their training activities. Project consultants were instructed to submit journals that reflected the diversity of agencies and individuals in their projects. Table 4 summarizes the agencies and job positions represented by these journal writers. It should be emphasized that these journals did *not* constitute a random sample of ToT participants. They were accumulated over a period of 5 years, as individual projects were in progress, and in the absence of any data on national distribution patterns.

- *End-of-project evaluation forms.* At the end of the project, all participants completed an evaluation form to assess the strengths and weaknesses of the training experience. They were asked to identify agency factors facilitating or hindering their participation and to note the reactions of staff, parents, and children to the curriculum.

- *Debriefing notes.* High/Scope project consultants completed a debriefing form after returning from each of the 7 weeks of training. The forms elicited observations, from the consultant's perspective, about the workshop sessions, the participant characteristics, and the strengths and problems of each project.

Added to these three data sources from all 40 projects was a set of **chronological observations collected by an ethnographer** who attended the Ypsilanti #1 ToT project. This person joined training sessions and visited candidates at their home agencies when they conducted workshops with agency staff members. In addition, he interviewed the candidates about their activities and reactions to their ToT experience.

Data Analysis

The author performed a content analysis of the qualitative materials to identify issues and recurring themes across the participants, consultants, and ethnographer in the 40 projects. A process of triangulation was used in this analysis. Confirmation from two or more data sources (journals, final evaluations, debriefing notes, and ethnographic observations) was the determining

Table 3

ToT PROJECTS IN THE PROCESS ANALYSIS ($N = 40$ PROJECTS WITH 793 PARTICIPANTS)

Project	Dates	Number of Candidates	Number Endorsed	Project	Dates	Number of Candidates	Number Endorsed
Flint, MI	5/87–12/87	21	20	New York #3, NY	5/89–12/89	22	14
Detroit #1, MI	5/87–3/88	18	11	Phoenix, AZ[+]	6/89–2/90	24	20
Chicago #3, IL	1/88–10/88	18	12	New York #4, NY	6/89–5/90	28	18
Dayton, OH	2/88–12/88	19	17	Battle Creek, MI	7/89–4/90	19	18
Orangeburg, SC[+]	2/88–12/88	15	10	Sault Ste. Marie, MI[+]	7/89–6/90	12	10
Iron Mountain/Houghton, MI[+]	3/88–12/88	10	9	Portland, OR[+]	10/89–4/90	18	17
Miami, FL	4/88–2/89	22	16	Detroit #2, MI	11/89–5/90	13	10
Seattle, WA	4/88–2/89	21	19	Ypsilanti #2, MI[+]	2/90–5/90	16	15
New York #1, NY	5/88–2/89	22	14	Dallas, TX	4/90–2/91	26	23
New York #2, NY	6/88–2/89	15	12	Bakersfield/Fresno #2, CA[+]	5/90–1/91	9	7
Orlando, FL	7/88–6/89	36	32	San Jose #2, CA	5/90–1/91	22	14
Lincoln, NE[+]	10/88–7/89	24	21	Los Angeles #3, CA	5/90–1/91	21	19
Houston, TX	10/88–8/89	20	16	Sacramento #3, CA	5/90–1/91	27	24
Alpena, MI	1/89–11/89	14	12	San Bernardino, CA	5/90–1/91	18	16
Ypsilanti #1, MI[+]	2/89–5/89	12	10	Milwaukee, WI	6/90–3/91	24	23
San Jose #1, CA	2/89–12/89	27	21	Princeton, NJ[+]	6/90–4/91	24	16
Bakersfield/Fresno #1, CA	2/89–12/89	11	11	Ypsilanti #3, MI[+]	2/91–5/91	24	22
Los Angeles #2, CA	2/89–12/89	21	20	Atlanta, GA+	2/91–10/91	26	22
Sacramento #2, CA	2/89–12/89	21	18	Total for 40 projects		793	658
San Diego, CA	2/89–12/89	14	14	Mean		19.8	16.4
Riverside, CA	2/89–12/89	19	16	Percent of candidates endorsed			83.0
Long Island, NY	4/89–2/90	20	19				

Note. Numbering is used to denote the existence of multiple projects in the same geographic location, for example, Detroit #1 and Detroit #2. The symbol [+] denotes that a project drew participants not just from the city named but from a wider area across and/or outside the state.

Table 4

JOURNAL SAMPLE: DISTRIBUTION OF JOURNAL WRITERS BY
AGENCY AFFILIATION AND JOB POSITION ($N = 157$)

Variable	Number of Journal Writers	% of N
Agency		
Head Start	37	23.6
Public school	39	24.8
Nonprofit	73	46.5
For-profit	8	5.1
Total	157	100.0
Job Position		
Director or program coordinator	47	29.9
Education coordinator or curriculum specialist	36	22.9
Teacher trainer or consultant	32	20.4
Teacher	35	22.3
Other	7	4.5
Total	157	100.0

criterion for identifying **issues** within each project. **Recurring themes** were then defined as those issues, or topics, that were mentioned in the materials of at least 25 percent of the ToT projects under review. Because the participant journals were specifically selected to represent a project's range of participating agencies and because participants' journal comments were generated spontaneously rather than as responses to standard questions, projects as a whole, rather than individual candidates, were used as the unit of analysis.

A Note on the Objectivity of the Anecdotal Data

The formative function of any program is enhanced by participant feedback. In fact, self-examination is our responsibility in undertaking a large-scale dissemination initiative. Qualitative data are an exceptionally rich source of this valuable and instructive information. However, the objectivity of anecdotal data may be subject to question, even when accepted methods of triangulation are used. This issue was addressed in two ways in the process analysis. First, a distinction was made between those delivering and those evaluating the program. Training was carried out by consultants in the Foundation's Program Division; evaluation was conducted by staff in the Research Division. Second, we are fortunate in having another data set that can be used to measure the validity of the in-house findings and our interpretation of the results. A series of studies on the first High/Scope ToT project in the United Kingdom was conducted by an outside, independently financed team of researchers from Oxford University (Berry & Sylva, 1987; Moore & Smith, 1987; Sylva, Smith, & Moore, 1986). Using interview and observational techniques, the UK evaluators drew conclusions about the training process, as well as about teaching practices and child outcomes. Their findings, albeit with a much smaller sample,[6] confirm both the qualitative and the quantitative results in this more comprehensive ToT Evaluation. This congruence will be noted wherever appropriate in the Results section of this chapter on the process analysis, as well as in the reports of the quantitative investigations in later chapters.

Results

1. What Were Participants' General Reactions to the Training Experience?

Table 5 lists the percentages of projects in which recurring themes emerged as participants described the benefits and drawbacks of participating in ToT projects. Each of the issues they raised is discussed here:

Professional and personal growth　Candidates recognized that ToT was a unique opportunity to develop their professional and interpersonal skills. Although most came to the project with extensive backgrounds in the field, they stressed that no training prior to ToT had provided them with an organizing *framework* for integrating their beliefs about early childhood. Administrators of UK participants echoed this observation (Sylva et al., 1986), noting that a major benefit of the project was that it provided their agency with a consistent educational philosophy on which to base program decisions.

> I have thoroughly enjoyed my training! It has helped solidify my views on child development and the educational process. It has given me a *rationale* to support my strategies. (Ypsilanti #2 Candidate)

The project was particularly rewarding, for US and UK participants alike, because it combined developmental theory with *practical application.* Candidates remarked that graduate training too often stressed ideas in the absence of strategies for implementing them. The ToT project was further valuable because it gave the participants practical experience conducting training. The ethnographer remarked that the most noticeable change in ToT candidates was their strengthened ability to deliver workshops by the end of the project. Despite having training responsibilities at their agencies, most candidates had never studied adult learning as part of their own formal job-preparation.

---

[6]The series of UK studies examined 12 candidates, 9 endorsed High/Scope trainers, 44 teachers, and 36 children.

Table 5

PARTICIPANTS' GENERAL REACTIONS TO THE ToT EXPERIENCE
(N = 40 ToT PROJECTS WITH 793 PARTICIPANTS)

Issue	% of Projects Raising Issue
Professional and personal growth	
Hands-on application of training and curriculum principles	95.0
Theoretical framework for organizing early childhood beliefs and practices	82.5
Renewed sense of dedication and advocacy for the early childhood field	80.0
Opportunity to earn Continuing Education Units or college and graduate credit	40.0
Networking	
Moral support from consultant and other candidates	92.5
Formation of local early childhood networks	87.5
Technical assistance from other candidates	77.5
Joining (inter)national early childhood networks	27.5
Stresses of participation	
Worthwhile effort, on balance	100.0
Level of administrative support, which affected project participation and implementation at agency	100.0
Competing time demands from job, family, and ToT	92.5
Anxiety about endorsement, due to participants' internal standards or agency expectations	62.5

> The training has given me the specific tools and techniques to use in training staff to implement the ideas and philosophy in which I have always believed. High/Scope gives "substance" to the phrase "developmentally appropriate practice." (Long Island Candidate)

In a very literal sense, candidates were able to advance professionally. With the approval of an institution of higher education, candidates could earn Continuing Education Units (CEUs) or credits toward college- and graduate-level degrees. This issue might have arisen among an even greater percentage of candidates than the 40 percent indicated here. However, High/Scope did not get approval to offer CEUs or advanced credits until December 1989. Thus, only those candidates attending ToT projects that were in process or begun after this date knew about this professional opportunity.

Advances in theory and practice all took place within a broader context of *renewed dedication* to early childhood. Many candidates, as a result of their immersion in ToT, spoke of their increased energy for their jobs and for the field as a whole. The project broadened their horizons and made them conscious of the *advocacy* role they could play within their agencies and communities. After their involvement in ToT, candidates were eager to apply their new skills toward solving agency and district-wide problems.

> Another positive outcome was my immersion in early childhood issues facing my district and community. I feel my participation in the High/Scope project redirected some of my energy and efforts from parochial daily issues to more-general widespread concerns in our district. (Detroit #1 Candidate)

Networking Beyond their individual growth, candidates benefited greatly from the professional contacts they made through the ToT project. The content of these new linkages was twofold: Colleagues provided candidates with both *moral support* and *technical assistance*. In the area of moral support, candidates were vocal about the importance of the *High/Scope consultants as role models*. Consultants offered both inspiration and living examples of active learning in practice.

> Thank you [consultant] for all the support through modeling words, challenges, and "pushes" to do my best, provision of materials, and time to manipulate thoughts. How could any of the trainees *not* have internalized active learning as [the consultant] provided that kind of learning environment all the time. Thank you! (Lincoln Candidate)

Fellow candidates in the project were equally important in providing encouragement throughout the training. Given the rigorous training demands and challenges of bringing about changes at their agencies, participants were understandably discouraged at points throughout the year-long cycle. But regular discussions with other candidates convinced them that they were not alone in their problems, and *peer encouragement* helped them to persevere.

> I'm glad we have time each training week to talk with one another about concerns we have regarding our training. I feel sometimes that I'm the only one that has problems with High/Scope implementation, and after talking with my peers I realize I'm not alone. It helps me to brainstorm with them for ideas on implementation, and I'm all charged up and ready to go again! (Alpena Candidate)

ToT also created an environment in which technical assistance among colleagues blossomed. The UK evaluators described this phenomenon as "networking and learning together." During the sessions themselves, candidates shared information and training strategies during their peer presentations. But beyond the regularly scheduled ToT activities, candidates formed their own associations for *sharing skills among agencies*. They arranged to help train one another's staff and to combine their areas of expertise to improve the overall quality of early childhood programs in their community.

> Seven weeks with one group with a particular focus was delightful. We have formed professional partnerships that will continue, I am sure. Already, groups are beginning to engage others for site training. (Los Angeles #2 Candidate)

Both the scope and the composition of the networks reflected the diversity of the ToT participants themselves. For example, in some projects, there was a welcomed emphasis on *local linkages*, to strengthen practices within a particular delivery system. A good example of this was the Houston site, where a majority of the candidates were from the same school district.

One of the biggest accomplishments was the development of a strong networking system between the 14 instructional supervisors and four directors, who are all employees of the Houston Independent School District (HISD). During the last week they set up a plan to introduce the philosophy of active learning to all 1,033 pre-K, kindergarten, and special needs teachers. High/Scope is now supported by the District Administration Office and by all the superintendents and principals. Candidates formed committees to conduct workshops on a monthly basis. Their long-range goal is to have developmentally appropriate classrooms pre-K through second grade. (Houston Consultant)

In other projects, candidates emphasized the importance of the *state and regional networks* that emerged from their associations through ToT. The curriculum training allowed participants from various places to "speak the same language" and work toward the same goals for overall program quality and specific program practices. To a lesser extent, candidates were also inspired by the fact that High/Scope was a *national and international organization* devoted to early childhood education. The broad reach of the Foundation gave an added sense of importance to candidates' individual and local efforts.

One important aspect of this training is that it brought all the Education Coordinators of South Carolina Head Start together and finally got us into the same curriculum, same assessment procedures, and same training content. It also got us all on the same "wavelength"—we really became coordinated and united. (Orangeburg Candidate)

Belonging to the membership association is a good way to keep in touch with other endorsed trainers and receive the Registry newsletter. It is encouraging to know that we are part of a well-established organization with approximately 1,000 members, not only in the USA but also in other countries. (Princeton Candidate)

Stresses of participation   Notwithstanding the glowing reports about growth and networking, candidates were quite vocal about the difficulties they encountered as a result of participating in the ToT project. Because candidates were generally selected from the ranks of advanced early childhood professionals, many saw the project as a measure of their ability and integrity. Participants expressed their *anxiety about endorsement* to the consultants and among themselves. The pressure to succeed was often internal, the result of high individual performance standards. Sometimes the pressure was external, however, as when candidates sensed that their sponsoring agencies expected their endorsement in return for the financial investment in their training.

None of us wants to "fail" in this project. All of us want to "pass" with flying colors! (Alpena Candidate)

But the biggest source of stress for candidates was the *competing time-demands* of their regular jobs, their family obligations, and the comprehensive requirements of the ToT project. As the ethnographer noted, participants were generally chosen because they held senior positions at their agencies. Their importance to their organizations meant that they were attempting to fulfill their regular duties while taking on the additional assignments of the ToT coursework. It was common for participants to complain about the role

conflicts and the sheer shortage of time for accomplishing all their responsibilities during the extended project period.

> From one week to the next my schedule is unpredictable. I get high on
> performing High/Scope and then low because my other job responsibilities in-
> tervene. I find that I am always cramming to meet some deadlines because of
> the demands of the job and the High/Scope training. It becomes overwhelm-
> ing. (New York City #1 Candidate)

Stress could be exacerbated or eased by the degree of *administrative
support* that candidates encountered at their agencies. Virtually every ToT
project contained examples of both the *absence* and the *presence* of agency
support and of the impact of each on project participants. When support
was lacking, candidates struggled to find the time to complete their assignments and train their on-site staff. By contrast, when agency support was
forthcoming (in the form of concrete resources and release time, as well as
moral encouragement), participants welcomed it as an invaluable aid to
completing their training and utilizing it within their agencies.

> The recruitment packet states that the trainer will devote at least 50 to 60
> percent of the time to implementing High/Scope. Our district, however, makes
> many demands on us, and unfortunately, very little time is allowed us to
> spend on High/Scope. (Houston Candidate)

> The support of my boss really facilitated my freedom to experience High/
> Scope training. Without that encouragement, money, and release time, it
> would have been impossible. (Iron Mountain/Houghton Candidate)

Candidates who were vocal about stresses and difficulties were equally
likely to proclaim that on balance, their participation had been a *worthwhile
investment* of individual time and agency resources. They saw many potential benefits for themselves, their staff members, and the children and
families in their agencies. The rigors of training were evidenced by the 83
percent endorsement rate. Clearly, the High/Scope training did not confer
endorsement status on every participant who attended the full complement
of sessions. Yet even those candidates who chose to complete the sessions
without meeting all the other endorsement requirements often stated that
they still benefited from participating in the training process.

> I am excited about this training and being part of it. It is quite a challenge—
> a lot of work—both during the actual training sessions and "on the home
> front"—but it promises to be very worthwhile for children and adults alike.
> (Orangeburg Candidate)

2. What Was Participants' Self-reported Understanding of the Course Content?

Table 6 lists the percentage of projects in which participants shared insights
about various topics of ToT course content. These topics are divided into
curriculum principles for children and *training strategies* for adults. It
should be emphasized that candidates were not systematically tested on
their knowledge about the topics, nor were they formally asked to rate their

understanding of them. Rather, results in this section are based on the spontaneous insights that candidates offered in their journals and final evaluation forms. Each of the curriculum principles and training strategies in Table 6 is discussed here.

Curriculum principles for children

Active learning for children. The principle of active learning is fundamental to the High/Scope Curriculum. Not surprisingly, this principle elicited the largest number of comments from candidates. Giving children choices and opportunities for hands-on learning was seen as the essence of developmental appropriateness. Because this orientation was compatible with their own philosophy, candidates generally had no difficulty internalizing the basic tenets of active learning for children.

> Children learn when they are developmentally ready. Active learning gives children the opportunity to develop their own interests, talents, and goals. Active learning provides experiences that are developmentally appropriate, and children are best able to accomplish and retain what they learn and relate it to previous experiences and future goals. Children learn through hands-on activities, where children and teachers communicate with one another and parents become involved in their children's education. We as teachers need to design our programs to fit the children. (Lincoln Candidate)

Table 6

PARTICIPANTS' SELF-REPORTED UNDERSTANDING OF ToT
COURSE CONTENT (*N* = 40 ToT PROJECTS WITH 793 PARTICIPANTS)

Issue	% of Projects Raising Issue
Curriculum principles for children	
Active learning for children	87.5
Daily routine (plan-do-review)	82.5
Room arrangement and labeling	80.0
Key experiences	67.5
Adult-child interaction	60.0
Curriculum adaptations: multicultural, special needs, infancy through elementary age, children at risk	60.0
Materials and equipment	47.5
Child observation and assessment	30.0
Small-group time	27.5
Training strategies for adults	
Presenting workshops	87.5
Active learning for adults	82.5
Observation and feedback for adults	80.0

Daily routine (plan-do-review). Next to the underlying principle of active learning, candidates were most interested in the concrete features of the High/Scope Curriculum—how to structure the temporal and physical environment. They saw the daily routine as a system for ordering a child's experiences within an open environment. Candidates' insights reflected their understanding of the learning opportunities inherent in the plan-do-review sequence. Many stressed the importance of language development in an atmosphere that encouraged children to talk about their activities—future, present, and past. They also emphasized the value of a daily routine in giving children a sense of anticipation and control over the events in their world.

> The plan-do-review routine seems to create more interdependent relationships between adults and children in our setting, compared to last year. Plan-do-review sets up a required child-adult interaction which establishes patterns of reflection, critical to long-term successful learning and living. Merely selecting and playing without recall lacks a vital element for growth and development. (Dayton Candidate)

Room arrangement and labeling. Candidates were eager to learn about establishing the appropriate physical environment for the curriculum. They found the specific principles of room arrangement to be the easiest to communicate in their own training of agency staff. Arranging and labeling the room was a concrete way that teachers could begin to implement the High/Scope Curriculum. Candidates soon understood how the physical environment affected not only the surface appearance of the room but also children's choices, independence, social interactions, and confidence. Work areas or centers provided children with a conceptual framework for classifying objects and activities. As well as being a necessary preliminary to language and literacy skills, labels allowed children to take care of their own needs at work and cleanup times.

> Teachers motivate children when the room is stimulating, warm, attractive, and well equipped. Appropriate room-arrangement and labeling allow children to make decisions, carry out choices, be creative, solve problems, organize their time, make sense of their world, feel good about themselves, and develop at their own rate. (Dallas Candidate)

Key experiences. Responding to questions by the ethnographer, candidates characterized their knowledge of the relatively abstract key experiences as being less solid than their mastery of the more concrete features of the curriculum. Nevertheless, journal entries indicated that the concept of key experiences was appealing and challenging to ToT participants. They appeared to grasp the basic tenet that key experiences are essentially children's everyday learning opportunities. Candidates further understood the pervasive role that key experiences played throughout the daily routine. They saw how key experiences differentiate High/Scope's approach from more-directive approaches and at the same time align it with other developmentally based curricula.

> I realized that key experiences reach the *child's* interest, and unit-based approaches reach the *adult's* interest. (Orangeburg Candidate)

The key experiences make such good sense to me. They are a part of anyone's good teaching regardless of whether they are "High/Scope" or not. The film shown today demonstrates how ever-present they are in children's play. I can see how easily the key experiences can be reinforced by stories, large- and small-group activities, as well as adult interaction during work time. (Alpena Candidate)

Adult-child interaction. The focus on key experiences as the basis for providing learning opportunities was carried over into the general realm of adult-child interaction. Comments from candidates indicated that ToT helped them to seriously reconsider the adult's role in children's learning. Although most came from what they described as "child-centered" philosophies, they nonetheless recognized the extent to which they and their staff often controlled program activities. High/Scope encouraged them to redefine the adult from *directive teacher* to *facilitator*. They learned to place more emphasis on following a child's lead to extend learning.

Children will construct their own learning if allowed to do so. An autocratic, directive teaching style does not allow children to engage with materials and people in a way that is meaningful to them. Teachers who respect and support children's ideas and creative endeavors engage them in exciting learning experience by providing an environment full of developmentally appropriate opportunities. (Sacramento #3 Candidate)

Curriculum adaptations. The diversity of backgrounds of ToT candidates meant that projects and participants frequently wrestled with how to adapt the basic curriculum to the varied populations served in early childhood programs. It was not uncommon for candidates to enter training skeptical that High/Scope could be used within the particular constraints of their program. Yet, as they experimented with implementation strategies, candidates discovered that the curriculum was applicable with a wide range of children:

- *Multicultural/multilingual children*

  Because of the discussion at High/Scope, I have become more conscious of promoting a multicultural atmosphere in our classrooms. An important point is to integrate cultures into everyday activities, rather than having a once-a-week or once-a-month activity. Multicultural should be used in every phase of the schedule—circle time, small-group time, outdoor play, as well as holidays, foods, and customs. (Atlanta Candidate)

- *Special needs children*

  Handicapped children find life much easier [with High/Scope]. The individualization has changed the focus of adults and allowed children's strengths to surface. (Iron Mountain/Houghton Candidate)

- *Age groupings from infancy through the elementary grades*

  Active learning can be from anything and anywhere. You don't need the expensive educational toys. An infant or toddler playing with kitchen utensils is learning. (New York City #3 Candidate)

  I just finished teaching the Kindergarten-Grade 4 section for a week. It reaffirmed my belief in how great things *could* be in elementary schools. I was working by myself with a group of 22 students, multiage and multicultural. The projects the children developed were so exciting. The interaction among the children was amazing. I wish people could see the *depth* of learning that takes place when children are excited. They'd come back the next day with books from home, or resources they wanted to share, or their own objects to add to what we were doing. It was all very open-ended and a lot of learning took place. (Lincoln Candidate)

- *Children at risk of abuse and neglect*

  The child who comes from a chaotic home environment may have very little understanding of routine. The low self-esteem that comes from this kind of powerlessness is exactly the reason why elements of High/Scope, such as giving choices and planning one's own activities, are so important for our children. Gradually the child will discover in himself the ability to make a plan and will begin to get satisfaction from the things he can accomplish through his own planning and exploration. (Seattle Candidate)

Materials and equipment. Many candidates thought about materials and equipment within the general context of room arrangement and the physical environment. The relatively low place of *materials and equipment* on the list of curriculum topics may therefore be a misrepresentation of its importance to candidates. Participants did emphasize the increased use of real objects and recycled, or "found," materials in their programs. Moreover, they tied the choice as well as the organization of materials to opportunities for key experiences to occur.

> It is helpful to look at classroom materials and decide how to organize them from a child's point of view. What labels will be most appropriate and facilitate a child's understanding of the key experiences? I see how organizing the materials will be a natural way for children to practice classification, seriation, spatial relations, number concepts. (Iron Mountain/Houghton Candidate)

Child observation and assessment. Candidates were generally excited about approaching child assessment through observational techniques. They saw observation as a developmentally appropriate alternative to standardized tests. Participants noted that the High/Scope assessment tools, which are based on the key experiences, were particularly effective in focusing teachers on children's interests and strengths. The fact that many candidates were themselves still developing an understanding of the key experiences may have accounted for the relatively low incidence of reflections about the High/Scope observational instruments, which are based on the key experiences.

> In using the High/Scope Child Observation Record to heighten their observational skills, . . . teachers get excited about things they hadn't noticed before. This tool helps them to focus and formalize the notes made on each child. Observation is good early childhood practice and should be the primary assessment tool! (Houston Candidate)

Small-group time. It was somewhat surprising that candidates did not generate more insights about small-group time in the High/Scope Curriculum. However, understanding this topic in a sense required unlearning earlier stereotypes about working with children in small adult-led groups. Moreover, small groups in High/Scope are grounded on the key experiences and adult-child interaction strategies that support and extend children's interests. Given the multiplicity of areas that impinge on the concept of small-group time, it is perhaps understandable that most candidates did not yet feel confident of their implementation or training abilities in this area. Nevertheless, those insights that candidates did share offered evidence that they understood the distinction between the High/Scope small-group time and small-group approaches typical of other early childhood settings.

> I wanted my trainees to understand that *small-group time* does not mean the same as *small-group instruction*—a term used in the public schools to refer to all of the children sitting and doing the same thing, using the same materials, and listening to the teacher talk. From the opening activity, my participants got the message that facilitation rather than "teaching" was what small-group time was all about. (Lincoln Candidate)

Training strategies for adults

Presenting workshops. Consistent with ethnographic observations and UK self-ratings (Sylva et al., 1986), candidates described ToT as greatly improving their workshop skills. Agencies were supposed to sponsor candidates with both experience in and responsibility for training at their sites. In reality, however, participants varied greatly in their training background. While many were in fact experienced trainers, others were recruited because agencies anticipated using them in training capacities in the future. Regardless of their background, however, all found that ToT offered ample opportunity to develop their ability to work with adults.

> It has been especially useful to study the workshop format and practice it in training. We were forced to look at workshop techniques. This is the first time I've seen this topic studied and reviewed to this extent (and I've had a *lot* of formal education). I learned a great deal and now feel confident about presenting workshops. (New York City #3 Candidate)

Active learning for adults. Closely related to candidates' general workshop skills was their ability to actively engage staff members in curriculum presentations. The similarities between adult and child learning became immediately apparent when consultants modeled active versus passive strategies in the early ToT workshops. Just as candidates themselves benefited from being active learners, so too did the trainers in the workshops candidates offered at their agencies.

> The teacher that I work with had a breakthrough recently and [said] "I finally get it. You're helping me to learn the way you want me to help the children learn." I felt so good! (Phoenix Candidate)

> As I plan training, I need to remember how I can balance a presentation to involve participants. Just as we create active learning environments for children, we need to create them for the adults we are training. (Milwaukee Candidate)

Observation and feedback with adults. Because their training responsibilities also entailed on-site supervision, candidates were grateful for the introduction of High/Scope's observation/feedback procedure. Some candidates admitted to having little prior experience doing individualized training with teachers. Those who did were troubled by a lack of effective tools that would enable them to evaluate staff in a noncritical manner. Candidates realized that by focusing their observations on children's behavior in the classroom, teachers became much less defensive during feedback sessions. Instead, trainers and teachers collaborated on program improvements that resulted in a better learning-environment for the children.

> I learned some principles that will help me provide feedback in an effective, encouraging way. I have been so sensitive to the already-low self-esteem of some of my staff that it was difficult for me to make suggestions for improvement in a way that wouldn't deflate them further. The principle of observing the children as the means of getting to what is happening in the classroom and leaving behind the focus on the teacher is so sensible and practical. I'm really excited about the prospects of success with this model. (Dayton Candidate)

3. What Were Participants' Experiences in Training Their Staff?

Table 7 lists the percentage of projects in which each recurring theme emerged as participants talked about training staff members at their own agencies. Staff reactions ranged from enthusiasm to resistance. Having been prepared by ToT to deal with varied responses, candidates were able to record in their journals detailed examples of their successes and coping strategies. Reflecting on their training and implementation efforts, the candidates reported significant changes in the programs and people they worked with. Their training experiences and the outcomes they observed are each discussed here:

Staff enthusiasm for training   For the most part, candidates met with positive reactions from their own staff when they introduced the idea of on-site training. Despite some early misgivings about the time commitment, teachers and providers were enthusiastic about joining in the training endeavor. The candidates' own excitement about the training process and the High/Scope Curriculum seemed to be contagious, and staff members were eager to share in the benefits of training.

Professional development of practitioners. The source of positive energy cited most often by candidates was the practitioners' desire to further their own knowledge and professional growth. Just as the candidates themselves welcomed the opportunity to advance their skills, so too did their staff members appreciate this all-too-rare concern with their own development. Participants emphasized the low status of most early childhood practitioners. Many were hired with little formal training in child development or curriculum. Those who had preservice training were seen as not needing additional support or information to continue growing in their jobs. The High/Scope program acknowledged the importance of ongoing inservice training at all job levels.

> A great many of the family day care providers don't even know who Piaget is, let alone understand his concepts. But they do understand children and possess wonderful instincts. Training has the potential to enhance the skills and

Table 7

PARTICIPANTS' EXPERIENCES TRAINING STAFF MEMBERS
(N = 40 ToT PROJECTS WITH 793 PARTICIPANTS)

Issue	% of Projects Raising Issue
Staff enthusiasm for training	
Professional development of practitioners	95.0
Antidote to low morale and burnout	65.0
Sources of resistance to change	
Structured or academic orientation	82.5
Complacency or inertia	67.5
Strategies for overcoming resistance	
Developing grassroots support and ownership of new curriculum	92.5
Having patience and allowing time for change to occur	90.0
Identifying commonalities in old and new approaches	65.0
Training outcomes	
For programs	
Improved physical environment	85.0
Improved adult-child interaction	82.5
For staff	
Greater teamwork and agency coordination	90.0
Enhanced job commitment	80.0

> self-esteem of providers and perhaps help them to avoid burnout. It might even be an important step in eliminating the label *babysitter*—a label many providers use in referring to themselves. I cringe when I hear it. (Sacramento #2 Candidate)

Antidote to low morale and burnout. Closely related to the specific need for training was the general concern with counteracting the low morale found in many agencies. Daily stress combined with minimal salaries and benefits contribute to high rates of staff burnout and turnover in the day care field (Willer & Johnson, 1989). Candidates reported that administrators and staff members saw the training as a vehicle for improving staff attitudes. Training communicated the message that staff were valued members of an important field.

> The teachers got involved in High/Scope because the director wanted something to lift their morale. The training has helped to bring about an attitude change. The teachers are now more articulate about the developmentally appropriate activities that are key to nurturing children's learning. They observe children and use the information to plan an environment to meet individual interests and needs. (New York City #2 Candidate)

Sources of resistance to change   The process of institutional change inevitably meets with resistance, and the experiences of ToT candidates were not exceptional in this regard. Reasons varied from the personal to the organizational, but candidates most frequently cited two sources of resistance in their agencies. One was specific to the curriculum approach in that it pitted structured teaching against High/Scope's open framework. The other was more generic, reflecting a common tendency to continue with current practices rather than shake up the existing system.

Structured or academic orientation. Candidates were most likely to encounter opposition from those whose backgrounds were grounded in relatively structured approaches to early childhood education. Some favored an academic program because they saw their job as preparing young children to enter kindergarten and meet the requirements of the public schools. Often, they were responding to administrative and parental pressure as much as to their own philosophical bent. Many candidates worked with teachers who came from a special education background that advocated structured activities to redress specific deficits in the students they worked with. And across the board, candidates described teachers who were simply reluctant to give up the control they exercised in their programs. These staff members began training with the misconception that an open framework with choices meant chaos in the classroom—children running wild and doing whatever they wanted.

> The teacher shared the concerns she has for the 5-year-old children who will be starting school next year. She feels that they are not receiving enough "structured" work and won't be able to perform on the achievement battery test. It's so hard to get all these teachers away from workbooks and stencils, because that's what all the public school kindergartens are using. I'm also having trouble with the language and handicapped workers who are pushing children too fast. They are so concerned with structure that they can't see the High/Scope way! (Orangeburg Candidate)

Complacency or inertia. Even when they did not have reservations specific to the High/Scope Curriculum, teachers were still sometimes skeptical of undertaking a new program. To a certain extent, they were reacting to the implicit message that having to change meant their old methods were "wrong." Some simply resented the time and effort required to learn new ideas and implement the necessary changes in their classrooms. Long-time practitioners were especially reluctant to abandon practices they were familiar with. Candidates described a prevailing level of complacency in their agencies that made it difficult at first to encourage an open attitude toward learning about High/Scope. They found inertia a powerful force to contend with.

> One of the teachers for the 2-year-olds was resistant toward trying any of the things she saw in the filmstrip. She felt her children were just too young: "You can't do much of anything like that with my children." It's hard to let go of things you've been attached to for many years. It means risking a lot. (Seattle Candidate)

Strategies for overcoming resistance   The High/Scope ToT model is designed to help candidates explore multiple strategies for coping with on-site training problems. To encourage candidates to discuss the progress of on-site training and share ideas for addressing the common problems they encounter, an issues-and-review session was held the first morning of every training week. Some strategies discussed were these:

Identify commonalities in old and new approaches. As a starting point, candidates tried to find a common ground with their trainees. Agencies that sponsored candidates in High/Scope tended to already advocate developmentally based programs. Candidates were thus able to emphasize that current practices and the High/Scope Curriculum were philosophically compatible; teachers did not need to alter their basic beliefs about what was good for children. Instead the training helped teachers make their practices more consistent with their underlying beliefs. This emphasis on continuity between the old and the new also helped candidates reassure experienced teachers that their existing programs were not being judged as "bad." The message was that training would build on practitioners' existing strengths by observing program effects on children.

> The teacher's attitudes are in agreement with Piaget's philosophy that "children learn by doing." But she realized how teacher-directed and restrictive she had become. She began to allow for more choices in her centers and made more materials available. The teacher began to encourage children to problem-solve on their own and to refer children to one another. She began to show more interest in what the children were doing and to give them more support. (Alpena Candidate)

Develop grassroots support and ownership of new curriculum. The most effective strategy described by the candidates was to "let the curriculum sell itself." They reported that once a *few* teachers had tried *some* of the ideas in their own classrooms—and experienced success—these teachers themselves became High/Scope advocates. Candidates told of testimonials from teachers who were won over to the curriculum and then encouraged their peers to try it.

> When the room arrangement workshop was first presented, all the participants were hesitant to implement the ideas. Once they experienced the almost instant success through the creation of work areas and the freeing up of themselves, they were willing to implement the ideas on labeling. Many of my teachers now say they cannot remember what it was like before High/Scope. (Flint Candidate)

The advantage of developing support in this way was that it allowed the momentum for change to come from the teachers instead of from agency administrators; it created grassroots rather than top-down support. Candidates described a process whereby teachers and day care providers assumed *ownership* of the curriculum—making its implementation and dissemination their own responsibility. They saw a parallel between teachers relinquishing control of activities in the classroom and candidates "letting go" of the model during training. The result in both cases was greater participation and active involvement on the part of the learners.

> The Training of Trainers concept has emerged wonderfully with my staff. The two people involved in initial training have stepped forward to train two more staff members. They have not been assigned that task, but rather have assumed the responsibility. The sense of ownership and team building is emerging. The

self-confidence gained for all involved has been one of the best outcomes. (Detroit #1 Candidate)

Have patience and allow time for change to occur. Candidates acknowledged that one of the hardest axioms to accept was that change takes time. Given both their internal pressure to succeed and the external pressure to pass the endorsement requirements, candidates sometimes held unrealistic expectations regarding the timetable for and extent of change in their agencies.

> I have altered my attempts to change it all, teach it all. High/Scope has provided me with the information to decide which content is most relevant, appropriate, and useful in any given situation rather than trying to force all the change in a short period of time. Select a slice, a modifiable issue, then give support and allow time for change. (Dayton Candidate)

Once they acknowledged that patience was a productive strategy, candidates relaxed and in fact became more effective as trainers. They were less tense and put less pressure on the teachers in their training classrooms. Feeling less pressure, the staff were in turn less defensive and more willing to experiment with the new curriculum. Training taught candidates that novelty might bring rapid change—until the next innovation came along. But steady and consistent changes in curriculum practice, based on a solid rationale, were likely to be sustained over a longer period of time.

> The High/Scope implementation is slow, which I think is good. It has a better chance of working—like a diet! (Houston Candidate)

Training outcomes   Although the pace and level of implementation varied greatly over the course of the project, by project's end, virtually all the candidates had observed in their training at least some movement toward greater High/Scope implementation. They documented changes in the practices of the *programs* at their agencies; they also observed changes among the *staff* who attended the training.

PROGRAM CHANGES

Improved physical environment. Beginning concretely, candidates worked with agency teaching staff to change the physical characteristics of their programs. Participants observed curriculum implementation in such areas as room arrangement, labeling, variety and accessibility of materials, and consistency of the daily routine. Teachers in turn reported to their trainers that these physical changes created better learning-environments and eliminated such problems as traffic congestion and fights over toys.

> Classrooms with rows of desks have changed to environments with areas centered around children's needs. Teacher-dominated instruction has changed to active learning, exploration by children, and focusing on the children as decision-makers and problem-solvers. Language is a natural part of the learning process. The organization of the classroom promotes responsibility and a sense of community among the students. (Lincoln Candidate)

Improved adult-child interaction. Once the physical environment was restructured, candidates noted significant changes in the interpersonal environment of their programs. They reported that training increased staff knowledge of basic principles of child development, a finding confirmed by the UK research (Moore & Smith, 1987). As teachers observed and followed the children's interests, programs became less adult-directed and more child-initiated. One UK administrator referred to this change as a movement toward the "child option." Once staff felt less pressured to control and plan everything that happened in their programs, they were able to devote more energy to observing and supporting the children on an individual basis.

> The staff felt that the plan-do-review cycle helped them to learn their children's developmental level more quickly. They are now able to interact more positively with the children and have developed their skills in entering children's play, questioning techniques, and creating problem-solving situations which help children learn *how* to think rather than *what* to think. (Flint Candidate)

STAFF CHANGES

Greater teamwork and agency coordination. Candidates documented improved collaboration among staff member at all levels of agency operations. Supervisors noted similar results among UK practitioners (Moore & Smith, 1987; Sylva et al., 1986). In fact, some candidates saw this enhanced spirit of cooperation as the greatest benefit of their on-site training. They described many instances of *teamwork among teachers* that resulted from attending workshops together and all striving toward the same goals for children. The High/Scope Curriculum gave them a common language for describing what they saw and what they did. Within the classroom, the new curriculum helped teachers to develop *meaningful roles for aides* in the program. Assistants who were previously relegated to custodial roles were now encouraged to plan with children and to get involved in their activities at work time. Finally, candidates found that training resulted in *greater coordination within the agency* as a whole. Staff at all levels—from administrators to trainers to teachers—got caught up in the spirit of program improvement, and the training gave them specific tools for accomplishing their collective goals.

- *Teamwork among teachers*

  > The training has given staff an opportunity to see curriculum through similar eyes. When we go into the classroom, we can all look together at room arrangement, daily routine, active learning, etc. We all talk the same language now! (Orlando Candidate)

- *Meaningful roles for aides*

  > Before High/Scope training, the aides did mostly housekeeping duties and had a passive role, while the teacher directed the children. Since training the team, the lead teacher is comfortable as a facilitator and respects and uses the aides to their fullest involvement. (Detroit #1 Candidate)

- *Greater coordination within the agency*

  > Now the staff is a more cohesive unit concerned about the success of the total center. Coming together for High/Scope workshops has encouraged them to openly share ideas and learn from each other. Individuals are willing to accept responsibility and be accountable to strengthen the team. Recognition by both

peers and administration has bolstered the staff's confidence in themselves and their abilities. (San Diego Candidate)

Enhanced job-commitment. Training also proved to be a powerful instrument in countering the discouragement and burnout endemic to the early childhood field. The experience of teachers and providers appeared similar to the "renewal" that many candidates themselves underwent. The mere fact that their agency *offered* inservice training was significant in eliciting a return commitment on the part of staff. By enhancing their skills during training, practitioners gained in confidence and self-esteem. Candidates described teachers as being happy, excited, and challenged. Several participants felt that turnover rates were down because of the training. Staff remained with the agency as long as their personal and professional growth continued.

> Training has brought about a revitalization of the teachers. Staff seem happier, more challenged, and have a better sense of "what we do and why we do it." (Iron Mountain/Houghton Candidate)

> Even though by this time of year teachers are usually burned out, I think my staff are enthusiastic about next year and ready to explore the curriculum even further. All are returning, which is a good sign that they continue to find the situation rewarding. They feel more confident about what they can do. (Orlando Candidate)

4. How Did Participants Characterize Parents' Reactions to the Curriculum?

Table 8 lists the percentages of projects in which ToT candidates mentioned several common parental reactions to the High/Scope Curriculum. Some candidates worked directly with parents and recorded the reactions they heard and observed. Others reported the parental reactions that teachers told them about. Although some parents were skeptical and even negative toward High/Scope, most responded favorably to the changes they saw in the program and in their children. Impressed with the changes the program brought about in their children, parents began to implement many curriculum features in their homes. Trainers and staff members also noted that the training brought about changes in the parent-teacher relationship itself. Each of these issues surrounding parents is discussed here.

Parental support for the curriculum

Positive reactions. In every project, candidates reported that parents were pleased with the High/Scope Curriculum. Parents, immediately noticing such things as the new room arrangement and the activities their children began to share with them on returning home, were aware of the changes. Parental enthusiasm stemmed from two sources: teachers' excitement about being involved in a new program and children's evident excitement about going to school each day.

Table 8

PARTICIPANT REPORTS OF PARENTAL REACTIONS TO THE CURRICULUM
(*N* = 40 ToT PROJECTS WITH 793 PARTICIPANTS)

Issue	% of Projects Raising Issue
Support for the curriculum	
Positive reactions	100.0
Negative reactions	27.5
Parent involvement	
More volunteering in the classroom	80.0
Increased attendance at parent meetings	55.0
More materials contributed to the classroom	37.5
Understanding of child development	
Increased appreciation of active learning	85.0
Increased confidence in parental role	55.0
Carry-over to home	
More opportunities for children to solve problems and make choices	85.0
More parent-child language	55.0
More-consistent daily routine	52.5
Improved parent-teacher communication	
Teachers' openness to parental needs and concerns	40.0
Child observations as the focus for parent-teacher discussion	30.0

> Staff said the parents were very positive about the program. I think it is because of our increased communication, more parent input this year, a stronger and more developed curriculum, and positive team-teaching dynamics. (Seattle Candidate)

Negative reactions. Initial responses to the program were not always positive, however. In over a quarter of the projects, candidates reported that some parents were very concerned about the *lack of academics* in the High/Scope Curriculum. They wanted to know whether their children would be prepared with the basic skills they needed to enter kindergarten. Some parents also expressed their displeasure when children stopped bringing home make-and-take art projects. These *parents wanted products*—while teachers were shifting their orientation to process.

> At our first parent orientation meeting, parents wanted to know if the children would learn the alphabet, how to write, and if they would get homework. Many thought play was for home, not school. (New York City #4 Candidate)

> Parents in our district are used to the teacher who just left after 7 years. She was very tidy, very busy, very orderly. She spent all her time preparing the "goodies" for the children to make and take home. (Battle Creek Candidate)

Parent involvement   As enthusiastic parents learned more about the curriculum—and as skeptical parents began to see its benefits for their children—they both demonstrated their support by becoming involved in a variety of ways.

More volunteering in the classroom.   In 80 percent of the projects, candidates reported that the number of parents volunteering to work in their children's programs increased after High/Scope was introduced. Most rewarding was the fact that parents moved away from custodial functions and began to play *meaningful roles in the classroom.* As teachers learned the curriculum, they modeled different interaction styles for parents to adopt with the children. Parents were encouraged to plan and recall with children and to become actively involved in their play. They realized that the participation in the classroom played an important part in children's learning.

> Parents are now actively engaged with the children in the classroom. They don't spend their time preparing support materials for the staff or discussing outside social activities among themselves. They recognize that their role is not to correct the children, but to help the children solve problems by working through situations. (Sacramento #3 Candidate)

Increased attendance at parent meetings. Perhaps because of parents' interest and involvement, their attendance at meetings and workshops also increased. They took a more active role in requesting and organizing the meetings. Staff reported that parents were more vocal during the sessions, asking questions about the program and how they could extend its benefits at home.

> Parents became curious and wanted to know more about High/Scope. They asked for a workshop, and attendance was very high when we presented it. Parents now seem more involved and ask more questions. (Ypsilanti #2 Candidate)

More materials contributed to the classroom. After the workshops on materials and equipment, staff encouraged parents to bring items from home into the classroom. Parents responded by bringing useful throw-aways that could be recycled by use in the classroom and also by contributing real objects, such as utensils and tools, to the house and construction areas. Candidates noted that parents lingered longer when they brought their children to school, letting the youngsters decide where to store the new materials. Parents also contributed to the physical environment in other ways, for example, by building outdoor play spaces or helping teachers label the room.

> Parents play a real part of the choice of materials. Very often they will not only send them in with their children, but will make an effort to bring in the materials themselves. Parents feel appreciated when the children react and choose what area to put the materials in. How many parents would bring in textbooks?! (Battle Creek Candidate)

Parental understanding of child development

Increased appreciation of active learning. Workshops and classroom participation also increased parental understanding of child-development principles. Most strikingly, candidates found evidence that parents began to see the value of active learning for their children. Initial doubts about the lack of academics were overcome. Instead, parents appreciated the *importance of play in children's learning.*

> Parents have seen the value of play in learning about the world. They have seen how High/Scope deals with many conceptual skills that are prerequisites to the academics to come. The comment "All they do is play" is becoming a thing of the past as parents gain insights into the developmental appropriateness of High/Scope. (Iron Mountain/Houghton Candidate)

Increased confidence in parental role. Parents also gained new insights into their own importance in relation to their children's development. Candidates noted that parents sometimes lacked confidence because they did not know how and what to "teach" their children. With the emphasis on observation and active learning, parents felt more confident about following their children's lead. Parents gained confidence, once they saw their role as supporting rather than directing their children's acquisition of knowledge.

> As a result of several workshops I did on active learning and child management, parents are reevaluating the approaches they use with their children. They show new excitement about being parents and share more experiences with their children. (Ypsilanti #2 Candidate)

Carry-over to home

More opportunities for children to solve problems and make choices. Training and program involvement also resulted in parents providing more opportunities for active learning in the home. Candidates and teachers cited numerous instances of parents offering children choices, giving them more responsibility for personal care and household chores, and generally fostering independent problem solving. Parents were also more conscious of improving the range and accessibility of materials for their children's play.

> Parents realize they are already providing learning experiences for their children during the normal course of the day, e.g., setting the table or sorting the laundry. They are allowing their children greater independence in self-care, and some have provided child-manageable storage containers in their bedrooms. Parents are more accepting of letting the children explore and are not so concerned about "mess." (Sacramento #3 Candidate)

More parent-child verbal interaction. Parents reportedly extended their children's learning by using more open-ended questions and by talking to them more, in general, about their activities. Candidates felt that the increased use of language in the home was probably initiated by the children themselves. Because they were encouraged to talk about their plans and activities at school, children eagerly carried on these same discussions at home. Parents were reportedly delighted at how their children were opening up verbally.

> Parents reported that their children are now anxious to tell about what they did, how they did it, and why. The language skills have improved. Before

when parents asked, "What did you do in school today?" the child's answer would be "Nothing!" (Princeton Candidate)

A more consistent daily routine at home. Participants were also pleased that the curriculum's emphasis on a consistent daily routine seemed to be generalized to the home setting. Those who described the children they worked with as coming from "chaotic" homes were especially encouraged by evidence of increased organization in the family environment. Parents generally liked the idea of plan-do-review because they thought it would encourage their children to approach activities in a more thoughtful and orderly manner. Parents in the UK echoed these sentiments, describing their children as more organized and less subject to frustration and temper tantrums (Moore and Smith, 1987).

> The parents are enthusiastic about the concept of plan-do-review. They are using it at home and feel it will create more order in their children's lives. (Alpena Candidate)

Improved parent-teacher communication

Teachers' openness to parental needs and concerns. In addition to observing changes in parents' relationships with their children, many of the candidates felt that High/Scope helped to improve parents' relationships with program staff. They stated that going through the change process themselves sensitized the teachers to the concerns parents might have about the new curriculum. Moreover, teachers learned from their own evaluation experiences what it must be like for parents to attend a conference where their own child was being evaluated. Just as trainers learned to start with the positives and build from there, so too did teachers learn to open conferences by talking with parents about their children's strengths. The teachers' more sensitive approach made parents less defensive and more willing to bring their questions and concerns to teachers.

> The effective communication workshop was helpful in bringing out how difficult change can be for parents, too. During conferences, I now approach parents as partners in the process. Using observation/feedback principles as a guide, I began with positive things their children were doing and shared ideas on the children's interests. The parents all seemed to have a positive approach while talking to staff. They used to be abrupt. (Ypsilanti #2 Candidate)

Child observations as the focus for parent-teacher discussion. Communication between parents and staff members also improved, once they both began to view themselves as partners in promoting children's development. The introduction of High/Scope observation tools helped teachers to establish this positive relationship with parents. Teachers said the observations were a vast improvement over the meaningless numbers and comparisons of standardized tests. Moreover, the observational format enabled them to share specific anecdotes with parents. The care that teachers took with note taking conveyed the message that they were paying attention to what the children were doing. Observations gave both structure and content to parent-teacher conferences.

> Teachers were excited about using the observation information from anecdotal records to communicate with parents. The teachers have a much better attitude toward parent conferences, now that they have a way of talking about the children's progress. (Ypsilanti #3 Candidate)

5. What Changes in Children Did Participants Attribute to the Curriculum?

Table 9 lists the percentages of projects in which ToT candidates described various kinds of changes in children's behavior after the High/Scope Curriculum was introduced into programs. Candidates' reports were based on direct observations of children in the classroom as well as on teachers' comments during training and staff meetings. Candidates described children's behavior in three areas of development: socioemotional, interpersonal, and cognitive. Although the anecdotal nature of the data meant there was no indication of the *amount* of change, it was noteworthy that the *direction* of change was always seen as positive. Moreover, the same words describing children's progress appeared spontaneously in interviews with UK trainers and teachers (Moore and Smith, 1987). These participant observations of children's behavior are summarized here.

Socioemotional development

Independence. Candidates and teachers in every project noted an increase in children's independence and self-directed behavior after High/

Table 9

PARTICIPANT REPORTS OF CHANGES IN CHILDREN'S BEHAVIOR
(*N* = 40 ToT PROJECTS WITH 793 PARTICIPANTS)

Issue	% of Projects Raising Issue
Socioemotional development	
Independence	100.0
Self-confidence	80.0
Enjoyment of school	72.5
Interpersonal relationships	
Self-management	87.5
Cooperative play	87.5
Cognitive development	
Language	90.0
Problem-solving skills	77.5
Attention span	70.0
Creativity	67.5

Scope was introduced. They attributed these changes first of all to environmental factors, such as room arrangement and labeling. Children were able to find the materials they needed to carry out their plans and could put the materials away on their own. Candidates also felt that High/Scope's approach to teacher-child interaction encouraged children's *sense of responsibility* and *self-control*. Because children chose and planned their own activities, they were more likely to take the *initiative* in starting and following through during work time.

> The children are becoming more responsible in their behavior. Because of the room arrangement and labeling, the children are able to select materials and return them to the proper place without a lot of adult supervision. (Dayton Candidate)

Self-confidence. Participants further stated that because children could operate on their own, they gained in self-confidence. They took *pride in their own accomplishments* and had a more positive "I can do it" attitude when faced with a challenge. The open-ended nature of their activities meant that there were no "right" or "wrong" answers for children to measure their accomplishments against. Candidates also hypothesized that because children had a say in the organization and labeling of materials, they took greater *pride in the classroom* itself.

> Children felt confident to know they could manipulate the materials in any way they wanted. There was no "right" or "wrong" way. They have a better self-concept. "I can do it!" is expected now. (Sault Ste. Marie Candidate)

> Children are more actively involved, self-assertive, independent, and have more opportunities to develop their environment. They feel ownership of the classroom, show pride in their accomplishments, and can take care of their own needs. Their satisfied attitude and confidence just shine through! (Phoenix Candidate)

Enjoyment of school. Candidates used many terms to indicate that children had a better *sense of well-being* under the High/Scope program. They described children who appeared joyous, felt relaxed and comfortable in the classroom, exhibited enthusiasm about their activities, and were generally happy about being in school. Again, they attributed these positive attitudes to the fact that children experienced success carrying out activities of their own choosing.

> The children were excited to be in school! They felt more at ease with their classroom. They were comfortable with the choice of activities. They seemed to be more active and they were happier. (Houston Candidate)

> The children work in centers now with a specific purpose. They carry out plans to completion, and they are very happy. This happiness is reflected throughout their discussions, [in] how they get along with peers and adults, [and in] talking and explaining to their parents at pick-up time what their day was like. (Orangeburg Candidate)

Interpersonal relationships

Self-management. Another very common observation was that discipline problems decreased substantially. Candidates, staff members, parent volunteers, and even visitors to the classroom all remarked on the absence of behavior problems among the children. Participants offered several explanations for why High/Scope cut down on disciplinary incidents. Because children were busy working on activities that interested them, there was less boredom and aimless wandering around the room. In addition, because the curriculum stressed having adequate materials for all the children to use, they did not have to wait or fight over limited resources.

> Making their own choices and decisions has resulted in fewer behavior problems in the classroom. Because children are actively learning, there is no time for boredom. There is less crying, fighting, hitting, kicking, and "s/he has mine." (Orangeburg Candidate)

There were striking similarities between these subjective comments and the independent, objective data from the UK studies. Noting that rough-and-tumble play gave way to purposeful activity, Moore and Smith (1987) described the classroom scene as follows:

> The general picture with High/Scope is a sense of order and purpose—children taking a far more active part in their own learning, making their own decisions, and spending less time waiting to be told what to do, flitting or wandering aimlessly about, or being disruptive (p. 5).

Cooperative play. The curriculum encouraged teachers to refer children to one another to share ideas or obtain assistance. The apparent result, according to candidates, was an increase in cooperative play. Participants reported a correspondence between the decrease in peer conflicts and the increase in positive interactions among the children. Youngsters who were proud of being able to take care of their own needs were also more eager to help one another. Their independence and self-confidence led them to resolve more problems on their own without immediately turning to adults for help.

> The children appeared to be more patient when listening to one another and taking turns. Children supported and offered to help one another more. They also looked to one another to solve problems much more than before. (Ypsilanti #3 Candidate)

Cognitive development

Language. Enhanced verbal skills were high on the list of changes observed by candidates and staff members. Their consensus was that the High/Scope *plan-do-review sequence promoted language development* among the children. Participants stated that children enjoyed talking because open-ended questions focused on the activities that they themselves had chosen. Several candidates noted that even shy children opened up under this process. And in bilingual programs, children were motivated to talk because they too wanted to share the interesting things that engaged them during work time.

> Their language skills are building. They plan, carry out, and talk about their activities. Using open-ended questions has made even the shy children vocal. (Sault Ste. Marie Candidate)

> Teachers report that children are developing language skills in our bilingual (Spanish/English) environment at a rate that exceeds "time and content" of previous years! (Phoenix Candidate)

Candidates whose programs had been using the curriculum prior to ToT also commented that the High/Scope program appeared to prepare young children with the *literacy skills* they needed in public school. Contrary to their fears about the lack of "academics," parents and teachers of kindergarten and first-grade children were pleased with their readiness to read and write. Anecdotal reports indicated that such activities as planning, recalling, and representing actions with pictures and words were exactly the kind of pre-literacy skills that prepared children for the elementary grades.

> We had this curriculum in place last year. I have been getting feedback about our "graduates" who are in kindergarten and first grade. High/Scope's integrated approach to reading and writing during the planning and review times helped to give them a purpose for reading and writing, and experiences in these when they were ready. This allowed their language abilities to flourish, and helped them to succeed in school. (Bakersfield/Fresno #1 Candidate)

Problem-solving skills. Also consistent with the goals of High/Scope were observations that children developed problem-solving abilities. Again, "choice" was seen as a major factor in this development. Candidates stated that children were motivated to figure out solutions to the problems that emerged naturally as they engaged in activities of interest to them. Moreover, adults actively encouraged children to manipulate materials on their own and to explore relationships among these materials. Because children were not worried about arriving at the one correct answer, they felt free to experiment with the options that were appropriate to their level of thinking.

> Before High/Scope, small-group time was completely chosen by the teacher. After High/Scope, the teacher guided it. The children now explore and solve problems, instead of the teacher solving them all. When the children are each given an object, it makes them feel that they are a special part of what is going on, and they can explore the object and decide what they want to do with it. (New York City #2 Candidate)

Attention span. Candidates indicated that children also brought greater concentration to their problem-solving activities. Because activities were based on their individual interests and developmental levels, children naturally stayed with each activity for a longer period. Moreover, because activities did not have a predefined or "correct" endpoint, children were able to extend their play with adult encouragement and support.

> The children are staying with an activity much longer because it is more open-ended, and matches their interests and ability level. (Seattle Candidate)

Evidence that children are absorbed by activities they themselves choose also comes from the observational data of the UK research. Berry and Sylva (1987) noted that the vast majority (91 percent) of preschool-aged children were able to plan and carry out activities, spending between 10 and 15 minutes completing their initial plans. Furthermore, approximately 90 percent of this work time was rated as being "on task"—additional confirmation of the purposeful nature of the children's activities.

Creativity. Finally, participants reported that the High/Scope Curriculum allowed children to be more creative in their play. They thought that the open-ended nature of activities, combined with the variety of found materials and real objects, freed the children's imaginations. Youngsters were not limited to copying the teacher's model or using materials in a prescribed way. As a result, such activities as art, construction, and role play became increasingly spontaneous and inventive.

> Since the introduction of more "found" and open-ended materials in the classroom, I have seen children blossom into their own creativity. (Ypsilanti #3 Candidate)

> The children's art work is more imaginative. There is a definite increase in the amount of dramatic play, especially in the house and block areas. (Detroit #1 Candidate)

Summary of the Process Analysis Results

Table 10 summarizes participants' (1) general reactions to the training experience, (2) self-reported understanding of the curriculum and training content, (3) experiences training staff at their own agencies, (4) reports of parental reactions to the curriculum, and (5) observations about curriculum effects on children's behavior.

1. Candidates perceived training as an overwhelmingly positive experience. While acknowledging the difficulty of balancing training, job, and family obligations, participants concluded that ToT was worth the investment of time and energy. Major benefits included the following: a comprehensive theoretical framework for organizing beliefs and making practical decisions, enhanced understanding of developmentally appropriate practices with children and training strategies for adults, a professional network of colleagues with compatible philosophies, and a renewed sense of dedication to improving the early childhood field.

2. Candidates were secure in their knowledge of concrete curriculum principles and training strategies. They acknowledged needing more time to master abstract and highly technical areas. Candidates were comfortable with the concepts of active learning for adults and children, daily routine (plan-do-review), room arrangement and labeling, workshop techniques, and observation and feedback with staff. They were less sure of key experiences, curriculum adaptation with different populations, and child assessment.

Table 10

SUMMARY OF PROCESS ANALYSIS RESULTS

1. What were participants' general reactions to the training experience?

Benefits	**Concerns**
■ The benefits made the investment of time and energy worthwhile.	■ Balancing the demands of training, job, and family was stressful.
■ ToT was an opportunity for professional and personal growth. Theoretical framework Practical strategies Renewed dedication and advocacy	■ Candidates experienced anxiety about receiving endorsement.
■ ToT promoted networking among early childhood professionals.	

2. What was participants' self-reported understanding of the course content?

Areas of Stronger Understanding	**Areas of Weaker Understanding**
■ Curriculum concepts Active learning for children Daily routine (plan-do-review) Room arrangement and labeling	■ Curriculum concepts Key experiences Small-group time Curriculum adaptation Child observation and assessment
■ Training strategies Presenting workshops to adults Observation and feedback with adults	

3. What were participants' experiences in training their staff?

Positive Experiences and Successes	**Negative Experiences and Problems**
■ Enthusiasm exceeded resistance. Professional development of practitioners Antidote for low morale	■ Doubts arose about High/Scope's lack of academic structure. Inadequate preparation for kindergarten Loss of teacher control in the classroom
■ Candidates successfully applied strategies to overcome resistance. Identifying commonalities between old and new approaches Developing grassroots support and ownership of High/Scope Curriculum Allowing time for change to occur	■ Staff showed complacency and inertia. Change as a negative judgment on previous practices Resentment about the energy necessary for change
■ Training improved program quality. Physical and interactive environment	
■ Training improved staff relationships.	

4. How did participants characterize parents' reactions to the curriculum?

Positive Reactions	**Negative Reactions**
■ Positive reactions far exceeded negative reactions.	■ Parents were concerned about lack of academic structure. Worries about children's readiness for kindergarten

Table 10 continued on next page

Table 10 (continued)

SUMMARY OF PROCESS ANALYSIS RESULTS

---

4. How did participants characterize parents' reactions to the curriculum? (continued)

Positive Reactions   **Negative Reactions**

- Parent involvement increased.

    More classroom volunteers

    Increased attendance at meetings

    Materials contributed to classroom

- Parent understanding of child development increased.

    Appreciation of the importance of play in children's learning

    Greater confidence in parental role

- Parents extended curriculum practices into the home.

    More choices for children

    More parent-child language

    More consistent daily routine

- Parent-teacher communication improved.

    Teachers more open to parental concerns

    Child observations providing positive and mutual focus for discussions

5. What changes in children did participants attribute to the curriculum?

Positive Changes   **Negative Changes**

- More independence and initiative   - None
- More self-confidence
- Greater enjoyment of school
- Fewer discipline problems
- More cooperative play
- Improved language skills
- Improved problem-solving skills
- Increased attention span
- More creativity and imagination

---

3. Candidates were generally able to counteract staff resistance to training. Successful strategies included stressing the continuity between new and former practices, developing grassroots support, allowing time for change to unfold, and enabling staff to assume ownership of the High/Scope Curriculum. Candidates reported that teachers appreciated the opportunity to develop professionally through inservice training.

4. Despite initial misgivings about the lack of academic preparation, most parents eventually embraced the High/Scope Curriculum. Parent involvement increased in the program setting, and parents applied the principles of choice and daily routine at home. Teachers reported that the High/Scope emphasis on observational assessment made it easier for them to talk with parents about their children's progress.

5. Candidates and teachers attributed children's emotional, interpersonal, and social gains to the High/Scope Curriculum. They reported that children were more independent and self-confident, less disruptive and more cooperative with peers, more adept at problem solving and verbal expression, more able to sustain attention during tasks, and more creative in their play.

IV The Registry Survey

The 1989 Registry survey continued the Trainer Study by interviewing a national random sample of 203 endorsed High/Scope trainers an average of 32 months after they completed ToT projects. Results showed that endorsed trainers worked with an average of 25 teachers each and devoted one day a week to training activities. This means that based on the 1991 figure of 1,075 endorsed trainers, an estimated 26,000 teachers nationwide have received training in the High/Scope Curriculum. High/Scope may have reached as much as 6 percent of the early childhood practitioners as a whole, and 12.5 percent of that portion serving low-income children. Survey data suggest there are over 13,000 High/Scope programs in the United States today, nearly half of them achieving advanced levels of curriculum implementation.

Purpose

The Registry survey (Larner & Schweinhart, 1990) was the second piece of the Trainer Study. It answered the broad question of what happened at sites in the months and years after participants completed their ToT projects. Trainers were interviewed about their backgrounds, work settings, and job responsibilities, and about the approaches they used when working with teachers. The Registry survey thus provided a picture of inservice training from the trainers' perspective.

Procedures

The Sample

The Registry survey was conducted with a random sample of 203 early childhood professionals who had successfully completed ToT projects. Subjects were identified using the *High/Scope Registry 1989 Directory*, a complete listing of all those who as of March 1989 had been endorsed to conduct training in the High/Scope Curriculum. From the 410 trainers in the continental United States, researchers drew a random sample of 240 and were able to interview 203, or 85 percent of the sample. Interviewers were unable to reach 33 people (some of whom had been trained 7 or 8 years earlier) and could not arrange interview times with 4 other sample members. No one whom we contacted refused to be interviewed. The sample thus contained approximately half of all the endorsed High/Scope trainers at the time of the study.

Table 11 describes the Registry survey sample. The 203 trainers, who came from 19 states and the District of Columbia, represented all regions of the country. The regional distribution of the 203 trainers was comparable to the regional distribution of Registry members as a whole. Sample members came to training with varying levels of motivation and knowledge

Table 11

DESCRIPTION OF HIGH/SCOPE REGISTRY SURVEY SAMPLE ($N = 203$)

Variable	Number	Percent
Response rate		
Trainers in random sample	240	100
Trainers who completed interviews	203	85
Trainers not contacted	33	14
Trainers unable to schedule interviews	4	1
Trainer's region of current residence		
Northeast (CN, MA, NY, NJ, MA, PA)	31	15
South (AL, AR, DC, KY, MD, MS, OK, TX, VA)	34	17
Midwest (IL, MI, OH)	75	37
West (CA, CO)	63	31
Trainer's circumstances of enrollment in ToT project		
Assigned by supervisor to attend ToT	117	58
Volunteered to attend ToT	78	38
Assisted in organizing ToT	8	4
Trainer's knowledge of High/Scope prior to ToT		
Little or none	57	28
General exposure	55	27
Reading High/Scope materials	19	9
Attending High/Scope workshop	47	23
Other	25	12
Trainer's year of High/Scope endorsement		
1982 to 1985	25	12
1986	36	18
1987	56	28
1988 to 1989 (March)	86	42

Note. At the time of the Registry survey, trainers had, on average, been endorsed for 32 months ($SD = 17$). The median duration of endorsement was 30 months.

concerning the High/Scope Curriculum. On average, 32 months had passed since their endorsement. The distribution of the 203 trainers with regard to their endorsement years reflects the timeline and pace of ToT projects, which began gradually between 1982 and 1985 and picked up rapidly thereafter. It is important to remember that although the Registry survey did not include participants endorsed after March 1989, both the telephone interviews and the program observations reported in later chapters were conducted in 1991 and included sites whose trainers attended more-recent ToT projects. It should also be noted that while the survey results are an accurate gauge of past and current training activities, they cannot be used to project the future activities of endorsed High/Scope trainers.

Instrumentation

Research staff developed the High/Scope Registry Survey, a 47-item telephone interview consisting of closed- as well as open-ended questions. The interview covered the following six areas:

- *Background information*—Trainers provided information about how long they had worked in the early childhood field and job positions they had held.

- *Exposure to High/Scope prior to training*—Trainers described their familiarity with High/Scope before training and explained how they learned about the ToT project they attended.

- *Positions held since endorsement*—Trainers described the agencies and positions they had worked in following their High/Scope endorsement.

- *Training activities*—Trainers described in detail the amount and nature of the training they had done from the time of their endorsement until the present time.

- *Other training approaches*—Trainers indicated whether they used training approaches other than High/Scope and whether their agencies used nonendorsed trainers to provide inservice training to staff members.

- *Educational background*—Trainers gave information about their educational background and early childhood training.

Data Collection

Endorsed trainers were interviewed on the telephone by members of the High/Scope research staff who had interviewing experience. Responses were recorded by hand. Each interview took approximately 45 minutes to administer. Some respondents were interviewed during the day at their work setting; others preferred to be called at home in the evening.

Results

Agency Characteristics

Since agencies sponsored trainers to participate in ToT, knowing trainers' agency affiliations at the time of endorsement helped us gauge the extent of organizational commitment to developing trainers as an in-house resource. The wide variety of sponsoring agencies indicated High/Scope's

Table 12

AGENCY CHARACTERISTICS REPORTED BY REGISTRY
SURVEY SAMPLE (*N* = 203)

Variable	No. of Trainers Reporting	Percent of Trainers Reporting
Type of agency		
Head Start	101	50
Public school	54	27
Private nonprofit	36	18
Private for-profit	5	2
Other	7	3
Program schedule		
Full-day sessions	53	28
Part-day sessions only	84	44
Both full- and part-day sessions	52	27
Other (home-based programs)	1	1

capacity, as of early 1989, to generate funds to reach out to various segments of the field. Table 12 shows the proportion of endorsed trainers representing each of the major sponsors of early childhood programs: Head Start, public schools, and both nonprofit and for-profit private agencies.

Half of the trainers endorsed by March 1989 were from Head Start programs. Several factors accounted for this high percentage. Head Start's funding, staffing structure, and scheduling all promoted inservice training. Further, there was a history of strong ties between High/Scope and Head Start that emphasized the consonance between the High/Scope Curriculum and the Head Start Performance Standards. (*Note:* As a result of funding shifts and active recruitment of other agencies, Head Start accounted for a smaller percentage of the endorsed trainers in 1991 than it did in 1989. Although exact figures are not available, Head Start accounted for 32 percent of the sample in the Teacher Study reported in Chapters 5 and 6.)

Public schools served as the institutional base for over a quarter of the trainers who were interviewed. Like those sponsored by Head Start, public school programs tended to have a sufficient portion of their budgets set aside for training activities. Another fifth of the sample (the 18 percent in nonprofit and the 2 percent in for-profit agencies) worked in private child care settings, which were almost exclusively center-based programs. The limited reach of High/Scope into child care, especially into home-based programs, was not surprising, given the restrictions on funding and staff time in these agencies. High rates of staff turnover in child care may also have discouraged administrators from making substantial investments in training. The very lack of a central administrative agency for many of these programs further curtailed access by High/Scope recruiters. Nevertheless, increasing awareness of the need for training, coupled with expanded contacts by High/Scope, did add to the representation of private program settings in subsequent ToT projects.

Trainer Characteristics

The ToT Prospectus recommends but does not require that agencies sponsor participants with college-level backgrounds and early childhood experience. Survey results in Table 13 show that these qualifications were met in almost all cases. The vast majority (88 percent) had at least 4-year college degrees, and half (51 percent) of the trainers had graduate degrees. Moreover, 70 percent had either an early childhood degree or credential, and 60 percent had attained at least a 4-year college degree along with some specialization in early childhood. Trainers' experience in teaching and training was equally high, averaging 16 years of work with children under age 6, and 8 years of conducting training. This strong background enabled participants to take full advantage of the fairly intense demands of the ToT projects. Their professional standing was also likely to give them influence within their agencies and credibility with the teachers they trained.

Turnover rates for staff in early childhood agencies are problematic. They are estimated to range from 17 percent in Head Start (Bloom et al., 1991) to as high as 41 percent in day care centers (Whitebook et al., 1989). However, this study documented that higher level professionals, such as those who participated in ToT, are more likely to remain active practitioners. Overall this was a relatively stable group, with only 2 percent leaving the early childhood field. (*Note:* Of the 33 random sample members who could not be reached, it is not known whether they left the field or moved to new locations but remained within the field.) Sponsoring agencies got a good return on their investment in ToT: 78 percent of the endorsed trainers remained with the same agency in either the same position (72 percent) or a different position (6 percent). Moreover, of the 26 percent who changed jobs either within or across agencies, half moved into positions of greater authority—supervising programs or expanding their training roles.

Job Titles and Responsibilities

Table 14 summarizes the data on the positions and roles filled by endorsed High/Scope trainers. Most (42 percent) were administrators who owned or directed programs; this included those responsible for supervising one or more centers within a larger system. The next-largest group (22 percent) were involved in training and curriculum oversight. Those in the Head Start system were typically called education coordinators; those working in other contexts were referred to as curriculum specialists, child development supervisors, or resource teachers. Only 11 percent of the trainers held jobs specifically titled teacher-trainer or consultant, perhaps reflecting the comparative novelty of this role in the early childhood field. Of the remaining trainers, 15 percent were teachers and 10 percent held other positions, such as college instructor, licensing agent, speech therapist, or social worker.

Job responsibilities also varied for the group. It was encouraging that 85 percent were specifically responsible for training, although most carried

Table 13

TRAINER CHARACTERISTICS REPORTED BY REGISTRY
SURVEY SAMPLE ($N = 203$)

Variable	Number	Percent
Highest level of education		
High school	6	3
Associate's degree	19	9
Bachelor's degree	74	37
Master's degree	99	49
Doctoral degree	5	2
Specialized training		
Credential/degree in early childhood	142	70
College and early childhood training	122	60
Years of experience in early childhood		
5 yr or less	13	6
6 to 10 yr	38	19
11 to 15 yr	47	23
16 to 20 yr	53	26
21 yr or more	52	26
Median = 15 yr		
Mean = 16 yr ($SD =$ 7)		
Years of experience training teachers		
2 yr or less	36	17
3 to 5 yr	55	27
6 to 10 yr	59	29
11 to 15 yr	31	15
16 yr or more	22	11
Median = 6 yr		
Mean = 8 yr ($SD = 6$)		
Professional plans for 5 years into the future		
Same job	75	37
Administration, advocacy	28	14
More teacher training	41	20
More direct service	24	12
Leave practice for more education, retirement	34	17
Job stability since High/Scope endorsement		
Same agency, same position	146	72
Same agency, different position	13	6
Different agency, still early childhood	40	20
Other (left early childhood, retired)	4	2

Table I4

JOB TITLES AND RESPONSIBILITIES OF TRAINERS
IN REGISTRY SURVEY SAMPLE ($N = 203$)

Variable	Number	Percent
Job title		
Director or supervisor	84	42
Education coordinator or curriculum supervisor	45	22
Teacher trainer	22	11
Teacher	31	15
Other	21	10
Responsibilities		
Training teachers	173	85
Administrative tasks	146	72
Supervising other staff	114	56
Classroom teaching	53	26

other roles as well. In addition to conducting training, 26 percent regularly taught in the classroom, 56 percent supervised or evaluated other staff, and 72 percent performed administrative tasks (budgeting, purchasing, reporting). Table 15 summarizes the amount of time that trainers spent fulfilling each of these job responsibilities. On average, they devoted 20 hours to administration, 6 hours to classroom teaching, and 3 hours to other activities. Despite these other obligations, trainers still devoted an average of 8 hours (one day) a week specifically to training activities.

The amount of time devoted to training differed little across different kinds of agencies. Trainers in public schools averaged 7 hours per week, while those in Head Start and private programs averaged 9 hours. The contrast across job titles was sharper, however. Those who were specifically titled teacher-trainer or consultant spent 13 hours a week doing training. They were followed by education coordinators and directors (at 9 and 7 hours, respectively) and, lastly, by teachers (at just 4 hours per week). It is interesting to note the overall similarity between directors and education coordinators in their use of time. Both averaged 3 to 4 days a week doing administrative tasks versus only 1 day a week doing training. On the positive side, having administrators who were at least sensitive to the need for inservice training was an asset to staff development within organizations.

Training Activities With Program Staff

Tables 16 and 17 summarize the training accomplishments of endorsed trainers between ToT project completion and the interview.

As indicated in Table 16, trainers varied in the amount of training they did following endorsement. Some had worked with no staff members, while others had trained over 50 teachers and as many aides. On average, trainers

Table 15

AVERAGE NUMBER OF HOURS PER WEEK SPENT ON
JOB RESPONSIBILITIES ($N = 203$)

Variable	No.	Hours of Training Teachers	Hours of Administrative Tasks	Hours of Classroom Teaching	Hours of Other Responsibilities
Sample as a whole	203	8	20	6	3
Across types of agencies					
Head Start	101	9	21	5	3
Public school	54	7	17	10	3
Private center[a]	41	9	23	7	1
Other	7	6	26	0	3
Across job titles					
Director	84	7	28	2	1
Education coordinator	45	9	25	2	3
Teacher trainer	22	13	12	5	5
Teacher	31	4	7	25	1
Other	21	8	16	5	6

[a]*Private center* includes both nonprofit and for-profit. Because trainers in for-profit centers made up just 2 percent of the sample, they were grouped with nonprofits for this analysis.

reported working, in their original job positions, with 13 teachers and 12 aides. The 37 trainers with training responsibilities at subsequent jobs worked with an additional 12 teachers and 10 aides. The number of staff trained varied with agency size. Some trainers worked in large agencies, where they conducted training with a new group every year; others worked in smaller organizations, where a relationship was sustained with the same classrooms over a longer period.

Although the numbers trained varied widely, all the trainers reported using the same set of strategies they had learned in the ToT project (Table 17). They emphasized active learning through hands-on workshops with ample opportunity for participation and discussion; 93 percent of the trainers held such occasions, on an average of once a month, with 15 staff members in attendance. A smaller proportion (63 percent) also did annual presentations to introduce the curriculum to larger groups averaging 36 people. Trainers traveled to provide one-to-one follow-up after the workshop sessions; 83 percent made informal classroom visits, and 79 percent scheduled observation/feedback sessions on specific aspects of the curriculum.

From the perspective of a typical teacher in an agency, High/Scope training could be characterized as follows:

- Training lasted 1 year 9 months
- Training included one large-group presentation

Table 16

STAFF TRAINING ACCOMPLISHED AFTER HIGH/SCOPE
ENDORSEMENT ($N = 203$)

Endorsed Trainer's Training Situation	No. of Teachers Trained					Teachers Trained (Mean)
	0	1–5	6–10	11–20	21 or more	
First job ($n = 203$)						13
No. of trainers	37	53	47	36	30	
(% of n)	(18)	(26)	(23)	(18)	(15)	
Second job ($n = 37$)						12
No. of trainers	11	10	5	6	5	
(% of n)	(30)	(27)	(14)	(16)	(14)	

	No. of Assistants Trained					Assistants Trained (Mean)
	0	1–5	6–10	11–20	21 or more	
First job ($n = 203$)						12
No. of trainers	40	49	46	39	29	
(% of n)	(20)	(24)	(23)	(19)	(14)	
Second job ($n = 37$)						10
No. of trainers	9	10	8	5	5	
(% of n)	(24)	(27)	(21)	(14)	(14)	

- Training included nine hands-on workshops
- Training included one structured observation/feedback visit each month
- Training included three informal classroom visits each month

Together, the training activities comprised sustained inservice training and ongoing support for curriculum implementation.

Teachers' Mastery of the Curriculum

Change is a gradual process, and implementation happens incrementally. Endorsed trainers were asked to judge how far along their trainees were in mastering the curriculum and using its principles in their classrooms. Although trainers were in a sense judging their own training skills by assessing their trainees, interviewers nevertheless found them willing to be critical and objective when programs did not yet meet their high standards for High/Scope implementation. The trainers' reports of curriculum understanding and implementation are presented in Table 18.

Table 17

METHODS USED BY ENDORSED TRAINERS (*N* = 203)

| | Trainers Using Method | | | |
Method	No.	% of *N*	Frequency (Median)	Attendance (Mean)
Large-group presentation	128	63	1 per yr	36 staff
Hands-on workshop	189	93	1 per mo	15 staff
Observation-and-feedback visit	160	79	1 per mo	2 staff[a]
Informal classroom visit	168	83	1 per wk	2 staff

[a] A classroom visit typically involved 2 staff—a lead teacher and an aide.

Trainers indicated how many teachers had tried the basic curriculum components and how many were using them comfortably and effectively. As expected, classrooms were most advanced in using the concrete aspects of the program—room arrangement and daily routine. All had tried the arrangement and routine ideas, and the vast majority (89 percent and 80 percent, respectively) were using their ideas with confidence. The more abstract concepts of using key experiences and using child observation as the basis for assessment were still in the early stages. Although most (91 percent) of the trainers had introduced staff to the key experiences, just over half (56 percent) were using them on a regular basis to plan activities for the classroom as a whole and for individual children. Because High/Scope's child observation is organized around these key experiences, it is not surprising that the lowest rates of both preliminary (63 percent) and advanced (37 percent) implementation occurred here. These findings about curriculum mastery are consistent with both our process analysis (in this ToT Evaluation) and the UK evaluation (Moore & Smith, 1987), which found that trainers, as well as teachers, started with the curriculum's simple mechanics and built toward understanding its more complex developmental strategies.

To get a sense of implementation from another angle, researchers asked the endorsed trainers how many of their classrooms they would be willing to "show off" to visitors as good examples of High/Scope implementation. On average, trainers had worked with 13 classrooms and identified about 6 of them (45 percent) as meeting this stringent standard. These numbers were further evidence that trainers were able to look at their programs objectively and identify needs for ongoing training and support. Yet the trainers did not appear discouraged that implementation was short of the ideal in many settings. Their own ToT experiences had taught them that mastering ideas and changing practices was not an instantaneous process. They felt that teachers were open to learning about the curriculum and eager to move up on the scale of implementation.

Table 18

TRAINERS' ASSESSMENT OF TEACHERS' MASTERY OF
HIGH/SCOPE CURRICULUM (*N* = 203)

Curriculum Component	% of Teachers Trying Component	% of Teachers Effective With Component
Room arrangement	100	89
Daily routine	100	80
Key experiences	91	56
Child observation	63	37

Summary of Registry Survey Results

The Registry survey, documenting the activities of trainers an average of 2½ years after they successfully completed ToT projects, was the second part of the Trainer Study. Interviews with a random national sample of 203 endorsed trainers produced the following picture of this link in the dissemination chain:

1. Endorsed trainers are a highly educated and experienced group with long-term commitments to the field of early childhood education.

- 88 percent of endorsed trainers have 4-year college degrees; 51 percent have graduate-level degrees.

- 70 percent have an early childhood degree or credential; 60 percent have both college and early childhood training.

- 94 percent have worked in early childhood for over 5 years; 75 percent have more than 10 years of experience in the field.

2. Trainers spend an average of 1 day a week training staff.

- Most trainers also fulfill other job responsibilities.

- Approximately 3 days a week are spent on administrative tasks, with another day devoted to classroom teaching or other activities.

3. Trainers work with an average of 25 teachers.

- Trainers work with approximately 12 to 13 classrooms.

- In each classroom, they typically train one lead teacher and one assistant teacher/aide.

4. Trainers implement the training strategies they learned in ToT.

- Trainers conduct large-group presentations about once a year to introduce the curriculum.

- They hold monthly hands-on workshops for small groups of approximately 15 staff members.

- Training workshops are followed up with regularly scheduled observation-and-feedback sessions and frequent informal visits to each classroom.

5. A typical teacher receives more than $1\frac{1}{2}$ years of training in the High/Scope Curriculum.

- Training is characterized by one formal presentation, nine hands-on workshops, and, each month, one structured observation and three informal visits.

6. Nearly half (45 percent) of the classrooms using High/Scope were described by their trainers as reaching advanced levels of implementation.

- The vast majority have mastered the mechanics of room arrangement (89 percent) and the plan-do-review sequence of the daily routine (80 percent).

- Full implementation of more-abstract concepts, such as key experiences (56 percent mastery) and the use of child observation for assessment (37 percent mastery), takes a longer time to achieve.

Implications for the Dissemination Chain

What do the Registry survey findings tell us about the actual and potential spread of the High/Scope approach within the national early childhood arena? The implications of the dissemination chain, illustrated in Figure 1, are explored below.

1. The 1,075 trainers endorsed as of December 1991 have trained 26,000 teachers working in 13,000 early childhood programs. Nearly 6,000 (45 percent) of these programs are demonstration-level quality.

2. To date, High/Scope has reached an estimated 6 percent of the potential early childhood training professionals.

- There are currently 7.3 million 3- and 4-year-old children in the United States (National Center for Children in Poverty, 1990). Of these, 4.5 million (61.4 percent) are in early childhood programs (Willer, Hofferth, Kisker, Divine-Hawkins, Farquhar, & Glantz, 1991).

Figure 1

THE HIGH/SCOPE TRAINING OF TRAINERS DISSEMINATION CHAIN

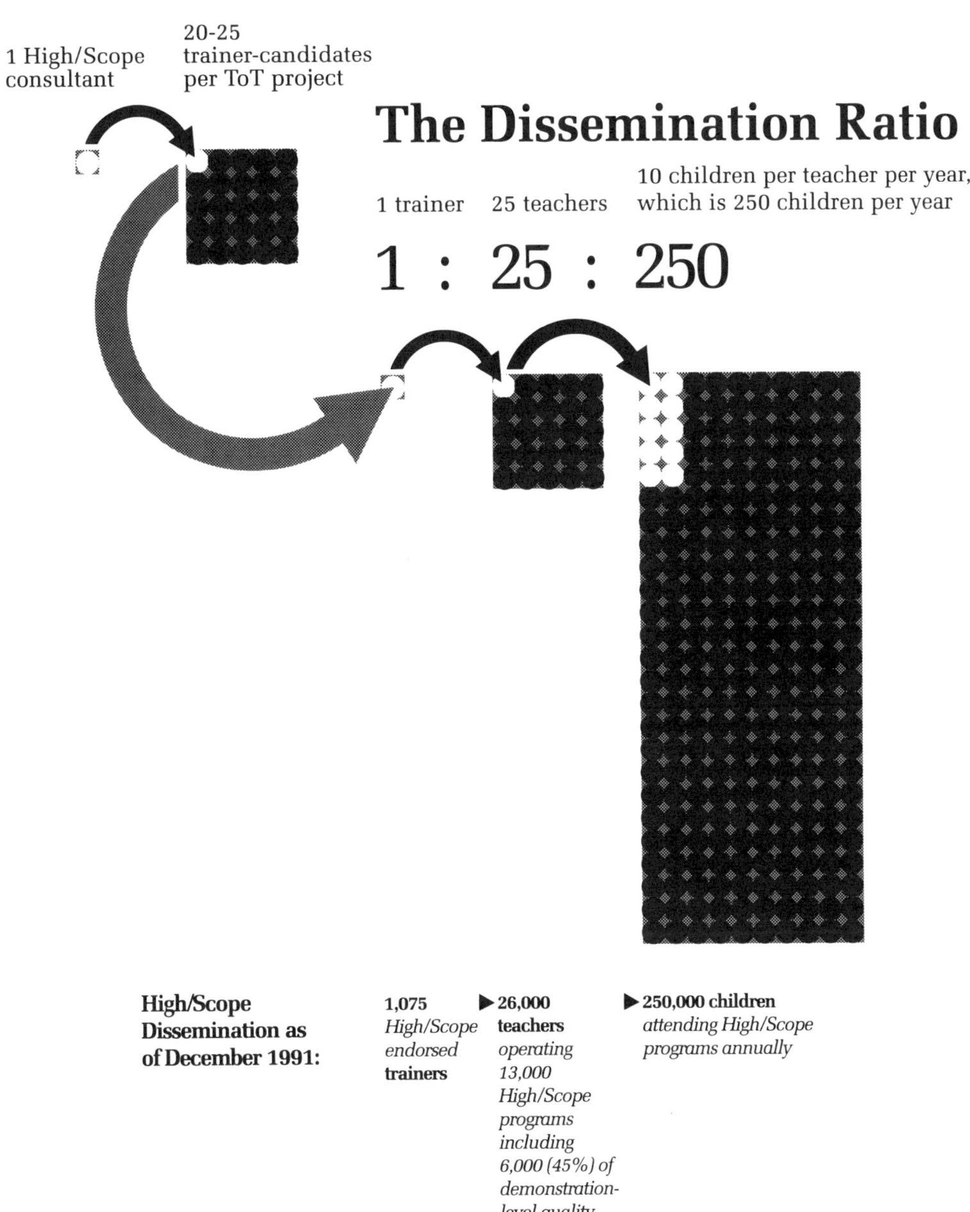

- At a ratio of 1 trainer to 25 teachers to 250 children per year, High/Scope would need to train an idealized target of 18,000 trainers to reach every teacher and every child enrolled in an early childhood program.

- The 1,075 endorsed trainers constitute 6 percent of this projected target.

3. To date, High/Scope has reached an estimated 12.5 percent of the potential early childhood field serving low-income children.

- There are 1.6 million poor 3- and 4-year-olds in the United States (National Center for Children in Poverty, 1990).

- To serve all eligible poor children in Head Start or other publicly subsidized programs, High/Scope would have to prepare 6,400 trainers (based on the above ratio of 1 trainer to 250 children).

- According to the Registry survey, approximately 75 percent of endorsed trainers are from Head Start (50 percent) and public school programs (25 percent) serving low-income children.

- The 800 (75 percent of 1,075) endorsed trainers working in programs for low-income children constitute an estimated 12.5 percent of this projected target.

V Teacher Interviews

Teacher interviews were the first half of the Teacher Study, conducted with 244 High/Scope and 122 non-High/Scope, or comparison, teachers. Sampling procedures resulted in high-quality programs for both groups, who probably represented the top 20 percent of early childhood practitioners in terms of education and experience. Despite this stringent standard of comparison, teachers in High/Scope programs received significantly more inservice training and administrative support than did teachers in comparison programs. High/Scope teachers attended more workshops and received more classroom visits, were more likely to cover curriculum and teaching issues during training, and saw their administrators as providing more training opportunities and encouraging more sharing among staff members. These results suggest that even good agencies can do more to promote the professional development of their teachers, particularly of teachers who are experienced and highly valued by the organization.

Purpose

The Teacher Study assessed the relationship between inservice training and program quality in 366 early childhood programs.[7] It looked at training and curriculum implementation in High/Scope programs and compared inservice activities and program quality at High/Scope and non-High/Scope sites. The evaluation was carried out in three states (California, Michigan, and New York) and used two research methods: (1) *teacher interviews*, which documented teachers' perspectives on inservice training and provided information on teachers' background and agency characteristics, and (2) *program observations*, a detailed and objective look at teaching practices. This chapter reports on the teacher interviews. The next chapter covers the program observations.

The teacher interviews launched the Teacher Study by looking at agency and training issues from the teachers' perspective. On the one hand, the evaluation was concerned with the successful transmission of the High/Scope Curriculum in the trainer-to-teachers link of the transmission chain. On the other hand, the evaluation was also interested in the general relationship between training and program quality. The sample therefore included both High/Scope and non-High/Scope (comparison) sites. The teacher interviews provided comparative data on teachers' background characteristics, the amount and type of inservice training teachers received, and teachers' perceptions of the organizational environments in which they worked. This information was subsequently related to program practices (Chapter 6) and child outcomes (Chapter 7).

---

[7]The term *program* refers to the physical operation that each teacher whom we interviewed and observed is responsible for. A program may be located in a school, center, workplace, or home. Thus a program may include but is not limited to the idea of a classroom.

Procedures

The Sample

The program sample—used for both the program observations and the teacher interviews—was drawn from regions around the country where High/Scope had done enough training to generate a sizeable number of trained teachers. Both groups—High/Scope and comparison—were selected from all licensed early childhood programs in the following three geographical areas:

- Southeastern Michigan and northern Ohio (hereinafter referred to as Michigan)

- San Francisco Bay Area (hereinafter referred to as California)

- New York/New Jersey metropolitan area (hereinafter referred to as New York)

At the time of sample selection, all the teachers involved in the sample were employed and had been working in their agencies for at least 6 months.

Selection of the High/Scope sample   To identify the High/Scope sample (i.e., programs that had teachers trained to use the High/Scope Curriculum), letters were sent to the 274 High/Scope trainers (endorsed as of September 1990) who worked in the three designated geographical areas. We explained that we were doing a follow-up study of inservice training and program practices and asked the trainers to identify the teachers with whom they had conducted High/Scope training. Of the 274 trainers who received our letters, 122 (44.5 percent) responded to our request.

To insure that teachers included in the High/Scope sample had in fact received High/Scope training, we asked endorsed trainers to provide us with the names of all teachers who met the following three requirements: (1) having attended at least four High/Scope workshops, (2) having received at least three on-site visits to discuss curriculum issues, and (3) having been employed at the agency at least 6 months. If more than one teacher in a given program had received training, we asked trainers to identify only the lead or head teacher in that program. The 122 endorsed trainers provided us with the names of 400 teachers who met these criteria, an average of 3.3 teachers per trainer.

Although the 3.3 average was less than the "13 teachers per trainer" finding from the Registry survey, three factors may account for the lower number in this phase of the study. First, trainers in the Registry survey had been endorsed for an average of 2.5 years, whereas over 38 percent of the trainers in our sample search had been endorsed for less than a year. Many of the latter group had thus been training for a shorter period of time. Second, the Registry survey asked trainers to report the total number of teachers they had worked with; the sample search asked trainers to identify only those who met the three just-mentioned minimal requirements regarding exposure to training and length of employment. Several trainers spontaneously noted in their replies that they were working with many more teachers who had not yet had this specified exposure to training. Finally, the knowledge that High/Scope might observe those teachers they named may also have caused trainers to be selective in identifying teachers.

We can speculate that (1) only half as much time had elapsed, on average, for endorsed trainers involved in the sample location compared with those in the Registry survey (i.e., 1¼ years instead of 2½ years); (2) endorsed trainers had therefore worked, on average, with half as many teachers (i.e., 7 instead of 13); and (3) endorsed trainers gave us the names of teachers working in the 45 percent of programs they regarded as demonstration-level examples of High/Scope (i.e., 45 percent of 7, or 3.2 names). By this reasoning, the average number of teacher nominations (3.3) per trainer is actually quite consistent with the results of the Registry survey. (For a further discussion of the factors affecting the teacher-nominating process, see the section of this chapter entitled The Study Sample in a National Context.)

Using the information provided by endorsed trainers, researchers next sent to administrators letters explaining in general terms the purpose of the study and asking permission for the teachers in their agencies to participate. The letter described the study as examining the relationship between inservice training and early childhood program practices. It did not say that we were specifically following up High/Scope programs and comparing them with non-High/Scope programs. The letter explained that we would be observing teachers in their programs and also doing a brief telephone interview. A list of the teacher names supplied by the trainer was included in the letter. Administrators were also asked to supply background information on the agency (e.g., type, size, population served) and to return this data with their consent forms. Similar letters were also sent to the teachers, explaining the general purpose and procedures of the study and requesting their participation. Teachers who consented were given, at the time of the observation, a gift certificate to buy a children's book for their program.

Selection of the comparison sample   In identifying the comparison sample, recruiters attempted to duplicate the proportions of various agency types that they anticipated having in the High/Scope sample. Projections were based on researchers' preliminary knowledge of the agencies already recruited and also on the variety and distribution of agencies documented in the Registry survey. Comparison sites were identified using three strategies. In the most successful approach, we obtained lists of all licensed early childhood facilities from the regulatory and referral agencies in each location. Second in effectiveness was asking High/Scope staff members and data collectors familiar with the three geographical areas for names of potential comparison sites. Our third strategy was asking the High/Scope trainers (when we contacted them by letter) to provide the names of administrators in agencies that had not received any High/Scope training.

Once prospective comparison programs had been identified, letters, including consent forms, were sent to their administrators. The comparison-group letters were identical to those sent to High/Scope program administrators, except that we did not propose a list of teacher names. Instead, comparison program administrators were asked to list for us the names of all teachers who had been employed at their agencies at least 6 months, a requirement that had also been established in selecting the High/

Scope sample (there were no minimal training requirements for comparison teachers, however). Once we received the administrators' signed consent forms and their lists of teachers, we were able to mail correspondence directly to individual teachers in the comparison programs.

Results of the selection process   The process of sample selection was time-consuming but ultimately successful. Where necessary, to secure responses from both administrators and teachers, initial letters were followed by second letters, postcards, and telephone calls. Persistence resulted in a high consent rate; fewer than 10 percent of those we contacted declined to participate in the study. Sites with High/Scope trainers were particularly pleased to have an ongoing connection with the Foundation, and the comparison agencies were also extremely cooperative. Perhaps the high response rate was at least partly attributable to our having gone through recognized channels (e.g., regulatory and coordinating agencies) to identify prospective participants.

Final sample   The resulting sample comprised 366 teachers and their programs,[8] two-thirds High/Scope and one-third comparison, drawn from a total of 129 agencies. Table 19 presents the characteristics of the programs in both the High/Scope and comparison groups.

The High/Scope and comparison groups were comparable on most background (agency and program) characteristics:

- *Agency type*—In each group, High/Scope and comparison, approximately one third of the programs were sponsored by Head Start and one third by private nonprofit agencies. The remainder were divided between public school and private for-profit sponsorship.

- *Population served*—Programs served primarily preschool children aged 3 to 5. About one fifth served 2-year olds, and several also cared for infants. School-aged children were served in only a few of the programs. The vast majority of both High/Scope and comparison programs served children from various ethnic minorities. Overall, significantly more High/Scope than comparison programs served children from minority, low-income, and at-risk groups. (Note, however, that the sample used in the Child Study reported later, in Chapter 7, was balanced on all these child characteristics.)

- *Program size*—Programs in the two groups were of comparable size and had comparable adult-child ratios. A median program size of 20 children, with fewer than 7 children per adult, indicated that the programs in each group met these important criteria for good-quality facilities.

- *Study participants*—The roles of study participants were also equivalent in the High/Scope and comparison groups. Most were lead teachers

---

[8]Three cases from the comparison group were observed but not interviewed. These 3 cases involved 1 teacher who declined to be interviewed and 2 teachers who could not be contacted to schedule an interview.

Table 19

CHARACTERISTICS OF THE PROGRAM SAMPLE

Variable	High/Scope (N = 244)	Comparison (N = 122)
Agency location by geographic region		
Michigan	38.9%	55.7%
California	32.8%	26.2%
New York	28.3%	18.1%
Agency type		
Head Start	31.6%	33.6%
Public school	17.6%	10.9%
Private nonprofit	37.3%	34.4%
Private for-profit	11.1%	15.1%
Other	2.4%	5.9%
Hours of program operation		
Full work day	40.3%	37.0%
Full school day	11.1%	8.4%
Part-day (morning or afternoon session)	14.4%	18.5%
Double part-day (morning, afternoon sessions)	34.2%	36.1%
Job title of person observed/interviewed		
Director and teacher	5.7%	8.4%
Lead teacher	57.8%	57.1%
Teacher	24.5%	32.1%
Assistant teacher or aide	11.9%	2.5%
Agency size[a]		
Median number of program sites	3	2
Mean number of program sites	11.6	8.4
Program size		
Median no. of children served	20	20
Mean no. of children served	24.3	22.7
Adult-child ratio	1 to 6.6	1 to 6.8
Programs according to age of children served		
Less than 2 years old	6.2%	6.7%
2 years old	18.5%	22.7%
3 years old	87.3%	81.1%
4 years old	92.2%	100.0%
5 years old	69.9%	65.7%
6 years old	2.9%	2.5%
More than 6 years old	0.1%	0.1%

Table 19 continued on next page

Table 19 (continued)

CHARACTERISTICS OF THE PROGRAM SAMPLE

Variable	High/Scope ($N = 244$)	Comparison ($N = 122$)
Programs according to ethnicity of children served[b]		
White	91.9%	96.1%
African American	91.4%	79.8%
Hispanic	88.5%	65.5%
Asian	75.8%	65.5%
Native American	56.6%	32.8%
Middle Eastern	69.1%	52.9%
Other minority	23.8%	14.3%
Programs according to service of at-risk children[c]		
Low-income	91.4%	78.2%
Physically/mentally impaired	79.5%	73.1%
At risk for abuse and neglect	71.4%	47.9%

Note. This table describes the characteristics of the *program sample* used for program observations and teacher interviews. The *child sample*, used in the Child Study (Chapter 7) and drawn from a subset of the Michigan programs, was balanced on all demographic variables.

[a]The number of program sites operated by agencies varied from a single site to statewide public school systems that operated over 1,000 sites.

[b]Significantly more High/Scope than comparison programs served minority children ($\chi^2 = 5.33, DF = 1, p < .05$).

[c]Significantly more High/Scope than comparison programs served low-income children and children at risk for abuse and neglect ($\chi^2 = 11.19$ and 17.96, respectively; $DF = 1; p < .001$).

or teachers. Several served simultaneously as program directors and teachers. More participants in the High/Scope group were assistants or aides, but this difference was not significant.

Because the study design did not involve a pre- and posttest of program quality before and after training, it was critical that the High/Scope and comparison samples be comparable on these background characteristics. The similarity of the two groups justified the assumption that any differences we discovered in program quality could reasonably be attributed to other factors, i.e., to differences in inservice training activities and curriculum implementation.

The Study Sample in a National Context

Although the two groups in this study represent virtually the same population, it cannot be said that they represent the population of early childhood programs nationwide. Overall, based on the descriptive and quantitative data analyzed in this study, we would conclude that both the comparison group and the High/Scope group represent the population of high-quality programs. On the one hand, this fact adds credibility to the study by making it harder for High/Scope to prove the benefits of its training and curriculum models. On the other hand, the relatively high quality of the programs raises the issue of whether the results of this study can be generalized to the early childhood field as a whole. How can we position the sample within this larger context in order to understand the meaning and the implications of our results?

We should emphasize that the evaluators did not *set out* to identify a sample of atypical program quality. As just described, teachers and their programs were identified by trainers and administrators through a neutral nomination process, without any stipulations regarding teaching skill or program quality. Comparison group nominations were based solely on a specified minimal length of employment, and High/Scope nominations, on the same specified minimal length of employment and specified minimal exposure to curriculum training. Theoretically, all teachers who met these criteria with a High/Scope or comparison agency could have been nominated for inclusion in the study. However, it is very likely that trainers and administrators provided the names of those they regarded as better teachers. Trainers, after all, would naturally want High/Scope to see their more successful efforts, and administrators would want their programs to look good in the eyes of outside observers. Although the total sample of 366 teachers and their programs in fact comprised a wide range of quality levels, the levels were better on average than those documented in early childhood surveys.

The resulting sample, while not representing the field as a whole, nevertheless does represent a considerable portion. It appears that the sample, on average, represents the *top fifth of early childhood teachers.* We reached this conclusion by comparing the characteristics of teachers in this study with those surveyed in the National Child Care Staffing Study (NCCSS). Table 20 presents this comparison.[9] The main reason for locating our sample within the top 20 percent is the data on formal education and years of experience. Approximately one fifth of the teachers in the NCCSS sample had at least a 4-year college degree and 10 or more years of teaching experience. Teachers in the ToT sample, averaging 16 years of schooling and 12 years of experience, corresponded with this top one fifth.

The education and experience differences between the two studies' samples were reflected in job positions and average salaries. In the NCCSS sample, over one third of the staff members were classified as assistant teachers or aides; the corresponding proportion in the ToT sample was less than one tenth. The NCCSS found an average hourly wage of $5.35 (1988 dollars), while teachers in the ToT study earned an average hourly wage of $9.49 (1991 dollars). This difference is reduced somewhat if we look only at the NCCSS teachers in nonchurch, nonprofit centers (i.e., a situation characteristic of 88 percent of the ToT sample). This subgroup of the NCCSS

---

[9]ToT numbers in Table 20 represent the combined High/Scope and comparison groups. Group differences on these variables are examined elsewhere in this chapter and in the following chapter.

Table 20

COMPARISON OF SAMPLES IN TOT EVALUATION AND NATIONAL
CHILD CARE STAFFING STUDY (NCCSS)

Variable	ToT Study[a] (N = 366)	NCCSS (N = 1,305)
Teachers according to formal education		
High school or less	5%	34%
Some college	27%	25%
College or graduate degree	68%	22%
Mean years of formal education	16	n.a.
Teachers according to years of early childhood teaching		
3 yr or less	7%	39%
3–10 yr	39%	42%
10 yr or more	54%	19%
Mean years of early childhood teaching	12	n.a.
Teachers according to job position		
Teacher	91%	66%
Assistant teacher or aide	9%	34%
Programs according to type of agency		
Nonprofit		
Head Start	32%	0%
Public school	15%	1%
Other (community, church, university-based, co-op)	40%	52%
For-profit		
Independent and chain	12%	47%
Stringency of licensing and regulatory oversight in sample locations[b]	MI = 2 CA = 3 NY = 3	Detroit = 2 Atlanta = 1 Seattle = 2 Phoenix = 1 Boston = 3
	Mean = 2.7	Mean = 1.8

sample had an average hourly wage of $6.40 and significantly more education and experience than teachers in for-profit centers. It is not clear if higher salaries attracted more-qualified teachers or if more-qualified teachers were rewarded with higher salaries. Nevertheless, more education and experience were prevalent in programs paying higher wages.

Comparisons of the ToT and NCCSS sampling techniques further suggest why the ToT sites were from the upper tier of early childhood programs. First, the types of agencies in the two studies may have made a difference. For-profit programs made up 47 percent of the NCCSS sample versus 12 percent of the ToT sample. It is likely that the subsidized (Head Start, public

Table 20 (continued)

COMPARISON OF SAMPLES IN TOT EVALUATION AND NATIONAL
CHILD CARE STAFFING STUDY (NCCSS)

Variable	ToT Study[a] (N = 366)	NCCSS (N = 1,305)
Programs according to hours of service		
Full-day (6 hr or more/day)	50%	100%
Double part-day (a.m. and p.m.)	35%	0%
Part-day (a.m. or p.m.)	16%	0%
Mean rating on the Early Childhood Environment Rating Scale (ECERS)[c]	5.3	3.6
Mean hourly wage[d]	$9.49 (1991)	$5.35 (1988)

Note. Categories in this table reflect comparable reporting levels in the ToT and NCCSS reports. Data on High/Scope and comparison teachers reported later in the ToT Evaluation differentiate on the basis of additional categories.

[a]ToT numbers represent the combined High/Scope and comparison groups. The two groups' differences on these variables are examined elsewhere in this chapter and the following chapter.

[b]NCCSS categorized stringency in words rather than numbers. ToT evaluators converted these narrative descriptions into a 3-point rating scale (1 = low, 2 = medium, 3 = high) and applied the scale to the ToT and NCCSS sites. Ratings should be considered an informal approximation, not a rigorous assessment.

[c]The ECERS is a 7-point rating scale. A rating of 5.3 on the ECERS is considered above "good." A rating of 3.6 is considered above "adequate."

[d]The mean hourly wage for NCCSS teachers in nonchurch, nonprofit centers was $6.40. In the ToT sample, 88 percent of the teachers worked in nonprofit programs.

school) and nonprofit programs, which accounted for 88 percent of the ToT sample, were more rigorously monitored than others. (For-profit agencies also tend to pay lower wages.) Second, as noted earlier, trainers and administrators in ToT agencies may have consciously or unconsciously chosen their better teachers to participate in the study; the NCCSS randomly selected staff members to be observed in the classrooms. Finally, although both the ToT study and the NCCSS identified participating agencies through licensing and regulatory bodies, the stringency of these oversight organizations may have been greater in the ToT study locations. When an informal rating scale is used to approximate the level of regulation (see footnote b in Table 20), it appears that programs in the three geographical areas in the ToT study may have, on average, been held to higher standards than those in the five areas in the NCCSS.

Final confirmation of the fact that ToT was sampling at a higher point along the quality continuum comes from the mean ECERS ratings in the two studies. ToT programs averaged ratings above "good," while those in the NCCSS averaged ratings above "adequate" (scores of 5.3 versus 3.6, respectively, on a 7-point scale). While not our original sampling intent, the domain of good programs may in fact be the most appropriate population for this evaluation. Programs at the low end of the scale, lacking the resources or interest for improvement, are an unlikely audience for our findings. This study speaks to the administrators, practitioners, researchers, and curriculum developers who want their good programs to become better programs—and who want proof of High/Scope's efficacy to accomplish this end.

Instrumentation

For both the High/Scope and the comparison samples, research staff developed a questionnaire, the High/Scope Teacher Telephone Interview. The instrument's development was guided by the central questions of the study as well as by relevant issues emerging from the literature on teacher characteristics, inservice training, and other determinants of program quality. The 35-item instrument had both closed- and open-ended questions. Teachers were asked about the following topics:

- *Agency and program characteristics*—Teachers provided information on the types of agencies employing them, the program features offered, and the populations served.

- *Background characteristics*—Teachers described their formal education and their early childhood training and experience.

- *Job title and responsibilities of teacher*—Teachers provided information about their job positions and the variety of roles they performed.

- *Inservice training*—Teachers described any outside training they had received, as well as the amount, type, and content of inservice training provided by their agencies.

- *Organizational climate and professional support*—Teachers responded to questions about the working conditions at their agencies, the salaries and benefits provided, and the rewards and frustrations of their jobs.

Data Collection

Interview data were collected from the late spring through the early fall of 1991. Trained High/Scope staff members and several of the Michigan program observers conducted the interviews (see Chapter 6 for a description of observer qualifications and training procedures). All were experienced interviewers. They were trained by a project assistant and conducted pilot interviews to standardize questioning and hand-recording methods. The interviewers were not told which sample group the teachers they interviewed belonged to, and program observers were never assigned to interview teachers in whose programs they had observed. Most interviews took place within a month of the program observations, although scheduling difficulties meant that several of the teachers were not contacted until a longer interval had elapsed. Teachers were telephoned at their workplaces during the day or at home in the evening, depending on their stated preference. Each interview lasted approximately 45 minutes.

Data Analysis

Frequency distributions provided descriptive data on the sample, and chi-squares and *t* tests were used to compare the High/Scope and comparison groups on interview variables (e.g., teacher background, inservice training, and organizational climate). Pearson correlation coefficients and multiple regressions were used to investigate the relationship of interview variables to observations of program quality (Chapter 6) and to child assessments (Chapter 7). Results are reported as significant at $p < .05$, two-tailed. In addition, results that are significant at $.05 < p < .10$ are reported as trends when they are corroborated by two or more findings on different measures.

Results

Teacher Background

Table 21 presents the education and experience of teachers in the two groups making up the study sample. Contributing to the relatively high quality of programs in the study were the levels of education and the amount of early childhood experience evident in this table. Large majorities of teachers in the study sample had college degrees (68 percent) and early childhood degrees or credentials (72 percent); over half (52 percent) had both college *and* early childhood training. Teachers in the study also averaged over 11 years of experience in the field. Table 21, in comparing the education and experience of teachers in the High/Scope and comparison groups, reveals some significant group differences, however. Teachers in the comparison group had more years of formal education, with a higher percentage having at least 4-year college degrees (80 percent versus 63 percent) and graduate degrees (42 percent versus 29 percent). Teachers in the High/Scope group had more early childhood experience overall (12 years versus 10 years), especially in lead teaching and assistant roles, although the comparison group tended toward more administrative experience.

Inservice Training

Tables 22 and 23 present group differences in inservice training at High/Scope versus comparison agencies. The first result that should be stressed is that *the great majority of agencies in both groups provided inservice training* for teachers—an average of over 45 hours per year. This finding is yet another indication of the high quality of the early childhood programs in this study.

Nevertheless, there were these *significant differences in the amount of inservice training*, all favoring the High/Scope group:

- More High/Scope than comparison agencies provided inservice training to teachers (94 percent versus 84 percent).

Table 21

GROUP COMPARISONS ON TEACHER BACKGROUND

Variable	High/Scope (N = 244)		Comparison (N = 122)		
	Mean	SD	Mean	SD	p
Years of early childhood experience	**12.2**	7.7	10.2	6.9	.014
Years of experience in early childhood job positions					
Program administrator	3.9	4.2	**5.6**	4.4	(.099)
Lead teacher	**7.3**	6.3	5.1	4.6	.002
Teacher/caregiver/provider	6.0	5.8	6.0	5.7	—
Assistant or aide	**5.6**	7.7	3.0	3.0	.001
Volunteer	3.5	7.6	2.8	3.8	—
Years of experience with school-aged children	5.8	8.3	7.0	9.2	—
Years of formal education	15.7	1.8	**16.4**	1.7	(.001)

	High/Scope	Comparison
Teachers according to years of early childhood experience		
Less than 1 year	0.8%	2.5%
1–2 years	5.4%	5.9%
3–5 years	17.9%	20.2%
6–9 years	18.7%	25.2%
10–14 years	22.4%	20.2%
15 or more years	34.9%	26.1%
Teachers according to highest level of formal education		
High school	5.1%	3.6%
Some college	32.3%	17.0%
Bachelor's degree	34.0%	37.5%
Master's degree	27.7%	42.0%
Doctorate	0.9%	0.0%

	High/Scope	Comparison	χ^2	DF	p
Teachers according to 4-year college degree	63.3%	**78.9%**	8.29	1	(.004)
Teachers according to early childhood degree	72.2%	70.7%	0.03	1	—

Note. In this table and in following tables, when there is a statistically significant difference, boldface type indicates the higher value. When the significant difference favors the comparison group, the *p* value is in parentheses.

Table 22

GROUP COMPARISONS ON TYPE AND TOPICS OF INSERVICE TRAINING PROVIDED BY AGENCY

Variable	% of High/Scope Agencies (N = 244)	% of Comparison Agencies (N = 122)	χ^2	DF	p
Availability of Training					
Agency provides inservice training	**93.9**	83.9	8.13	1	.004
Agency requires attendance at inservice training	**79.4**	58.8	16.04	1	.000
Types of Training					
Presentations by people from outside the agency	**85.9**	77.1	3.72	1	.053
Workshops by agency trainers/consultants	**83.1**	61.0	20.04	1	.000
Classroom visits (observation/feedback)	**74.4**	54.7	13.14	1	.000
Staff meetings devoted to curriculum issues	**73.7**	61.9	4.70	1	.030
Content of Training					
Child growth/development	69.4	61.5	1.87	1	—
Curriculum and teaching practices	**90.9**	70.9	22.40	1	.000
Supervised field work	17.4	18.3	0.00	1	—
Child assessment and evaluation	**74.8**	47.9	24.31	1	.000
Licensing/legal issues	**70.8**	60.7	3.25	1	.071
Parent involvement	60.3	53.0	1.46	1	—
Staff relationships	34.7	28.2	1.24	1	—
Professional issues	**48.3**	34.2	5.86	1	.016

- High/Scope agencies were more likely than comparison agencies to require attendance at inservice training (79 percent versus 59 percent).

- High/Scope teachers attended more agency-sponsored inservice training sessions in the previous year than did comparison teachers (31 versus 22 sessions).

There were also these *significant differences in the type and content of inservice training* sessions, all favoring the High/Scope group:

- Teachers in High/Scope programs had more workshops and more classroom visits from in-house trainers than did comparison teachers. They were also more likely to discuss curriculum issues at staff meetings and to have workshops by outside presenters.

Table 23

GROUP COMPARISONS ON INSERVICE TRAINING
ATTENDED BY TEACHER

Variable	High/Scope (N = 244)		Comparison (N = 122)		
	Mean	SD	Mean	SD	p
Number of agency-sponsored inservice training sessions per year	**30.5**	38.0	22.1	29.1	.022
Number of nonagency inservice training sessions attended per year	3.9	14.6	2.4	4.8	—
Number of hours of inservice training attended per year	47.5	52.5	42.0	51.4	—

- Inservice training in High/Scope programs was more likely to cover these topics: curriculum and teaching practices, child assessment and evaluation, and professional development of staff.

Table 24 presents group comparisons on how teachers used a 3-point scale to rate the importance of certain curriculum features. The features rated by the teachers reflect the issues stressed during inservice training and program implementation. Overall, on these 3-point scales, scores of both groups averaged 2.1 or higher. Despite this mutual "floor," we did find individual rating differences that were consistent with the High/Scope approach to both child and adult development. High/Scope teachers rated the following features as significantly more important in their programs than did comparison teachers:

- Arranging rooms according to interest or activity areas

- Children choosing their own activities

- Adult participation in children's activities

- Ongoing training, supervision, and evaluation for teachers

- Multicultural awareness

- Parent involvement

Finally, Table 25 describes how teachers defined the major *ingredients of good inservice training.* High/Scope teachers rated group discussion and follow-up significantly higher than did comparison teachers, and they tended to place more value on hands-on learning. Endorsed trainers learn to stress these active-learning components during High/Scope ToT projects. Perhaps because trainers emphasize these characteristics, teachers also see them as being important. High/Scope teachers also described themselves as being significantly more open to changing their practices, based on what they learned during inservice training. Their greater openness to change

Table 24

GROUP COMPARISONS ON TEACHERS' RATINGS OF IMPORTANCE OF
CURRICULUM FEATURES IN THEIR PROGRAMS

Feature[a]	High/Scope (N = 244)		Comparison (N = 122)		
	Mean	*SD*	Mean	*SD*	*p*
Room arrangement according to interest/activity areas	**2.9**	0.3	2.8	0.4	002
Consistent daily schedule	2.9	0.3	2.8	0.4	—
Children choosing their own activities	**3.0**	0.1	2.9	0.6	.001
Adult participation in children's activities	**2.7**	0.5	2.5	0.6	.000
Team planning by adults	2.7	0.6	2.6	0.7	—
Ongoing training for adults	**2.8**	0.5	2.5	0.7	.000
Supervision and evaluation for adults	**2.6**	0.6	2.4	0.8	.005
Regular child observation	2.8	0.4	2.8	0.5	—
Testing and screening	2.3	0.8	2.1	0.8	—
Multicultural awareness	**2.7**	0.6	2.5	0.7	.013
Parent involvement	**2.8**	0.5	2.5	0.7	.000

[a]Teachers rated the importance their program placed on each feature as 1 = little, 2 = some, or 3 = a great deal.

may be attributable to their more active involvement during training, as well as their greater opportunity to work out implementation issues during follow-up visits from on-site trainers. The coherence of the High/Scope Curriculum and its emphasis on *why* children benefit from its practices may also contribute to teachers' willingness to change their program approach.

Organizational Climate

Tables 26 and 27 present group differences in teachers' working environments. The variables examined included administrative support (as teachers perceived it), salary and benefits, and job satisfaction. Significant differences favored the High/Scope group on several of these organizational factors:

- Teachers in High/Scope programs rated administrative support higher than did those in comparison programs. Specific differences were in the areas of providing training opportunities and encouraging sharing among staff members.

- Benefits were significantly better in High/Scope than in comparison programs. High/Scope agencies more often provided health insurance

Table 25

GROUP COMPARISONS ON INSERVICE TRAINING FEATURES IMPORTANT TO TEACHERS

Feature[a]	High/Scope (N = 244)		Comparison (N = 122)		
	Mean	SD	Mean	SD	p
Theory/rationale behind the ideas	2.7	0.4	2.7	0.5	—
Presentation style	2.6	0.6	2.6	0.6	—
Opportunities to practice ideas during session (hands-on learning)	**2.8**	0.5	2.7	0.6	.095
Group discussion and sharing	**2.9**	0.3	2.8	0.5	.021
Follow-up sessions and workshops	**2.7**	0.5	2.4	0.6	.001
Follow-up classroom visits	2.5	0.6	2.4	0.7	—
Teachers' openness to change based on inservice training[b]	**2.6**	0.5	2.5	0.5	.039

[a]Teachers rated the importance of each feature of inservice training as 1 = not important, 2 = somewhat important, or 3 = very important.

[b]Teachers rated their openness to change based on what they learned during inservice training as 1 = not likely to change, 2 = somewhat likely to change, or 3 = very likely to change.

Table 26

GROUP COMPARISONS ON ORGANIZATIONAL CLIMATE

Variable	High/Scope (N = 244)		Comparison (N = 122)		
	Mean	SD	Mean	SD	p
Degree of Administrative Support[a]					
Provides training opportunities	**2.7**	0.6	2.5	0.7	.010
Encourages staff communication and sharing	**2.7**	0.5	2.5	0.7	.003
Secures resources	2.7	0.6	2.7	0.6	—
Approves of curriculum practices	2.8	0.6	2.8	0.5	
Provides overall support	**2.7**	0.5	2.6	0.5	.058
Hourly wage in dollars	9.7	4.2	9.1	4.6	—
Number of benefits offered by agency[b]	**4.2**	1.2	3.8	1.4	.015
Number of job rewards cited by teacher	1.5	0.7	**1.7**	0.8	(.013)
Number of job frustrations cited by teacher	1.7	1.0	**2.0**	1.1	(.038)

[a]Teachers rated administrative support on each dimension as 1 = not supportive, 2 = somewhat supportive, or 3 = very supportive.

[b]Types of benefits are listed in Table 27.

Table 27

GROUP COMPARISONS ON TYPES OF AGENCY-OFFERED BENEFITS

Benefit	High/Scope (N = 244) % of Agencies Providing	Comparison (N = 122) % of Agencies Providing	χ^2	DF	p
Health insurance	**86.4**	70.3	12.27	1	.001
Paid sick leave	**92.1**	85.7	3.00	1	.083
Paid holidays	86.0	79.0	2.34	1	—
Paid vacation	54.5	52.1	0.11	1	—
Child care/tuition	36.0	37.9	0.06	1	—
Retirement/pension	**55.8**	44.5	3.63	1	.057

(86 percent versus 70 percent), and differences on retirement plans and paid sick leave approached significance. Again, the somewhat higher percentage of public school agencies in the High/Scope group may have accounted for these differences. Overall, over 85 percent of the High/Scope teachers received health insurance, paid sick leave, and paid holidays. Over half had paid vacations and pension plans. These benefits compared favorably with the field as a whole and probably reflected the large number (88 percent) of ToT sample teachers working in nonprofit agencies. The National Child Care Staffing Study, for example, reported that whereas only 33 percent of *all* teaching staff receive health insurance benefits, 61 percent of those working in nonchurch, nonprofit centers have such benefits. Comparable numbers for retirement benefits were 17 percent (all teachers) versus 34 percent (nonchurch, nonprofit teachers).

- There were no significant differences in salaries in the two groups. Average hourly wages (over $9) were higher than one typically finds in early childhood (e.g., 77 percent higher than those reported for all teachers in the NCCSS 3 years earlier, and even 48 percent higher than those in nonchurch, nonprofit agencies). As discussed at the beginning of this chapter, higher salaries may reflect the higher levels of education, longer experience, and higher percentage of publicly funded or subsidized agencies in this sample relative to the national picture.

- The reasons for the degree of job satisfaction—ranging from the intrinsic reward of working with children to the frustration of inadequate program resources—were similar for the two groups. But the total number of rewards, as well as the total number of frustrations, was significantly higher among the comparison teachers. This finding may simply reflect the fact that comparison teachers took advantage of the interview to voice their feelings about their jobs. Because High/Scope agencies more regularly provide such opportunities for staff, teachers in the High/Scope group were less likely to use the interview for this purpose.

Summary of Teacher Interview Findings

Teacher Background

1. Teachers in the study sample (including both High/Scope and comparison groups) were highly educated and had many years of experience in early childhood education.

- Nearly 70 percent had 4-year college degrees, and over 70 percent had early childhood degrees or credentials; over half (52 percent) had both college *and* early childhood training.

- Teachers on average had 11 or more years of experience in the field.

- Comparisons with the NCCSS sample suggest that teachers in this study make up the top fifth of the early childhood profession.

2. Teachers in the comparison group had significantly more formal education.

- A higher percentage of comparison than of High/Scope teachers had college degrees (79 percent versus 63 percent).

- A higher percentage of comparison than of High/Scope teachers had graduate degrees (42 percent versus 29 percent).

3. Teachers in the High/Scope group had significantly more experience.

- High/Scope teachers averaged 12 years of experience versus 10 years for comparison teachers.

4. There was no significant group difference in the number of teachers with early childhood degrees.

Inservice Training

5. Over 90 percent of the agencies in the study provided inservice training for teachers.

6. The amount of inservice training was significantly greater in High/Scope than in comparison programs.

- Significantly more High/Scope than comparison programs provided inservice training (94 percent versus 84 percent).

- Significantly more High/Scope than comparison agencies required attendance at inservice training (79 percent versus 59 percent).

- High/Scope teachers attended significantly more inservice training sessions per year than comparison teachers did (31 versus 22).

7. The type and content of inservice training was significantly different in High/Scope versus comparison programs.

- Teachers in High/Scope programs had more workshops and classroom visits by in-house trainers than comparison teachers had.

- Teachers in High/Scope programs participated more in their training.

- Inservice training in High/Scope programs was significantly more likely to cover curriculum issues, teaching practices, child assessment, and professional development of staff.

- High/Scope teachers described themselves as significantly more likely to change their teaching practices, based on their training experiences.

Organizational Climate

8. Teachers in High/Scope programs rated administrative support higher than did teachers in comparison programs.

- High/Scope programs provided more training opportunities.

- High/Scope programs encouraged more sharing among staff members.

9. Teachers in High/Scope and comparison programs earned comparable wages.

- For the total sample, the average hourly wage was $9.49, which is 77 percent higher than that reported in the NCCSS 3 years earlier. Higher wages were attributed to the higher levels of education and experience of the ToT sample. The greater percentage of for-profit agencies in the NCCSS (47 percent versus 12 percent) may also account for this difference in the average wages of the NCCSS and ToT samples.

10. Benefits were significantly better in High/Scope than in comparison programs.

- High/Scope programs provided better health insurance and retirement benefits than comparison programs did.

- For the total sample, benefits were better than one typically finds in the early childhood field. Approximately 80 percent of the agencies provided health insurance, about 90 percent had paid sick leave, and over half offered paid vacations and retirement benefits.

This chapter devoted considerable discussion to sampling issues: why the teachers in this study represented the top 20 percent of their profession and how this sample fit within the broader context of the early childhood field. The fact that the comparison as well as the High/Scope group comprised high-quality programs actually added credibility to the research by making it that much harder for us to prove that our training and curriculum models provided significant benefits. And although the sample does not represent the field as a whole, it does constitute an appropriate audience for this study—good programs seeking to become better programs. The results suggest that even good early childhood agencies can do more to promote the professional development of their teachers, particularly those who are highly qualified and valued by their organizations. Our results may also suggest a strategy for upgrading programs lower down on the continuum, i.e., by starting at the top and raising quality levels, as a whole, through training. The next two chapters address the question of whether providing a coherent system of inservice training does in fact improve program quality and enhance the development of young children.

VI Program Observations

Program observations completed the Teacher Study with a detailed and objective look at teaching practices in the 244 High/Scope and 122 comparison programs. Results confirmed that though the comparison programs were of high quality, High/Scope programs were nevertheless rated significantly higher on many factors. Teachers in High/Scope programs were better than those in comparison programs at organizing the physical environment, encouraging independent thought and action, and using adult-child interaction to promote children's reasoning and language skills. The only area in which comparison programs outscored High/Scope programs was in supporting children's gross-motor development. Across all programs, the organizational-climate variables of wages, benefits, and administrative support were positively and significantly associated with program quality. Program quality was also significantly predicted by teachers' formal education, inservice training, and teaching experience. Other studies have found that experience by itself does not result in good caregiving. The current results suggest that experience obtained in the context of a good program environment can provide the role models and support needed for professional development.

Purpose

Program observations were the second part of the Teacher Study. The observations specifically documented the extent to which High/Scope settings were implementing the curriculum and, more generally, compared the level of program quality at High/Scope versus comparison sites. The program observations were important for several reasons. First, they assessed whether a primary goal of ToT had been met—whether ToT promoted program practices that used an open framework and were developmentally appropriate for children. Second, they enabled us to look across settings at how teacher background, inservice training, and organizational climate relate to the level of program quality. Third, the observations provided the basis for examining the impact of teaching practices on the development of the young child.

Procedures

The Sample

The sample for the program observations was the same as that used in the telephone interviews with teachers. There were 366 early childhood programs[10] drawn from a diversity of agencies and locations in Michigan,

---

[10]As in the previous chapter, *program* refers to the physical operation that each teacher whom we interviewed and observed is responsible for. A program may be located in a school, center, workplace, or home. Thus a program may include but is not limited to the idea of a classroom.

California, and New York. Two thirds of the sample were High/Scope programs, and one third were comparison programs. A complete description of the sampling procedures and sample characteristics was provided in Chapter 5.

Instrumentation

The following three observational measures were used to assess program practices. Although there is some overlap in these measures, they nevertheless focus on program quality from complementary perspectives.

The Arnett Global Rating Scale (Arnett)   The Arnett is adapted from a teacher-rating instrument used in the National Child Care Staffing Study. It consists of a series of 31 statements describing teacher behaviors (e.g., "speaks warmly to the children" or "exercises control over the children") and requires observers to rate the incidence of each behavior on a 4-point scale ranging from "not at all" to "very much." For the present evaluation, the items themselves were essentially left intact. However, the researchers added to the development of the measure by supplying operational definitions for each of the 31 items. These definitions were necessary to establish inter-observer reliability and provided a basis for interpreting the ratings. In addition to the individual-item scores, an Arnett total score was derived from the mean rating across all 31 items.

The Early Childhood Environment Rating Scale (ECERS)   The ECERS is a widely used observational tool for documenting the quality of early childhood programs. Observers used 32 seven-point scales to rate programs on six dimensions: personal care routines, furnishings and display, language and reasoning experiences, fine- and gross-motor activities, creative activities, and social development. In addition to item and subscale scores, an ECERS total score was derived from the mean rating across all 32 items.

The High/Scope Program Implementation Profile (PIP)   The PIP is a generic adaptation of an instrument developed by High/Scope to assess the degree to which programs adhere to the curriculum model.[11] For the ToT Evaluation, several small changes were made in the measure. All labels that identified the form as a High/Scope assessment were removed. Three items containing curriculum-specific references were reworded to capture the generic quality of interest. All three items dealt with the plan-do-review sequence and were rewritten to describe opportunities for children to plan, carry out their own ideas, and recall with others what they did during free-choice periods. One section of the PIP, on adult-adult interactions, was omitted entirely. These six items (e.g., team planning, use of child observation instruments, inservice training) were instead covered during the teacher

---

[11] To avoid possible observer bias from using an identifiable High/Scope instrument, the PIP was temporarily renamed the Program Observation Measure (POM) during the period of data collection.

interview, using questions rather than an observational format. Observers used the resulting 24 five-point scales of the PIP to rate programs on three dimensions: physical environment, daily routine, and adult-child interaction. In addition to item and subscale scores, a PIP total score was derived from the mean rating across all 24 items.

In sum, the program areas addressed collectively by the three observational instruments were these:

- Physical environment of the program

- Daily routine

- Adult-child interaction

- Opportunities for learning in all areas of development

- Teacher style and sensitivity to children's needs

Table 28 presents the correlations of the subscales and total scores among the three program observation measures for the sample as a whole. All the relationships were significant at $p < .001$, with correlations ranging from .24 to .86. These correlations indicated that the instruments collectively assessed common components underlying program quality. The high magnitude of intercorrelations may have also reflected the fact that the same observer used all three measures simultaneously. Yet the unaccounted portion of the variance indicates that each instrument brought unique dimensions to the measurement process. The Arnett was strongest in capturing the overall emotional tone of adult-child interaction in each setting. The ECERS provided the most detailed assessment of the physical structure of the programs—the adequacy of the equipment and how the materials were used throughout the day. The PIP also looked at the program environment, but it added an in-depth examination of the content of adult-child interactions. This third observational measure also allowed the evaluators to assess the "fidelity" of programs in implementing the High/Scope Curriculum.

Data Collection

Selection of observers   In all, 25 observers were recruited: 6 from California, 5 from New York, and 14 from Michigan. The largest number were hired from Michigan because we anticipated easier access to local sites and also because we planned to train several of the Michigan observers to conduct the child assessments. We used a variety of strategies to recruit observers from all three geographical areas. Job announcements were mailed to colleges that had relevant departments (education, early childhood, child development). Advertisements were also placed in college newspapers and in the major newspapers of each metropolitan area. Response to the announcements was high, resulting in a large pool of applicants to select from. Members of the research staff interviewed prospective observers by telephone and followed up their references. Because we wanted observers to be as objective as possible, applicants with anything more than a minimal familiarity with the High/Scope name were screened out. In all professional respects, the qualifications of the observers we hired were impressive. They

Table 28

CORRELATION OF PROGRAM OBSERVATION MEASURES,
TOTAL SAMPLE (*N* = 355 TO 362)

Variable	Arnett Total	PIP Physical Environment	PIP Daily Routine	PIP Adult-Child Interaction	PIP Total
Arnett Total	—	.40*	.35*	.46*	.47*
ECERS Personal Care	.24*	.52*	.42*	.52*	.54*
ECERS Furnishings	.38*	.73*	.46*	.59*	.69*
ECERS Language	.51*	.62*	.60*	.81*	.79*
ECERS Motor	.49*	.57*	.40*	.68*	.63*
ECERS Creativity	.38*	.74*	.57*	.73*	.78*
ECERS Social	.47*	.74*	.57*	.72*	.80*
ECERS Total	.51*	.80*	.60*	.81*	.86*

Note. Analyses of subscale and total scores were based on complete cases only. A maximum of 11 out of 366 cases were lost: 3 to 7 from High/Scope and 2 to 4 from the comparison group. There were no significant differences between complete versus missing cases by group on agency background characteristics.

*All correlations were significant at $p < .001$.

ranged from recent graduates to retired teachers, and all had experience both as practitioners and as classroom observers.

Observer training   The observers were all brought to the High/Scope Foundation for a week of intensive training in the use of the instruments. They were told that the project was a general investigation of inservice training and program practices in early childhood education. The High/Scope Curriculum and its training model were not discussed, and observers were discouraged from asking questions about the Foundation's work or talking with other staff members during their stay. During their week-long training, the observers had extensive practice using the instruments. Both videotapes and live settings were employed in this practice. Differences in ratings were discussed, and decision-making rules were clarified and documented. Observers also learned procedures for scheduling observations and delivering data to High/Scope.

Inter-observer reliability   For each of the three instruments, inter-observer reliability was computed in live settings under realistic observation conditions. Observers were paired with High/Scope staff members to determine the percentage of agreement (i.e., the number of agreements divided by the total number of agreements and disagreements) on scale items. Percentages were calculated for both *exact agreement* (identical ratings) and *close agreement* (within one point on the rating scale) for each item. In addition, after returning to their home locations, observers were paired with one another

Table 29

INTER-OBSERVER RELIABILITY ON PROGRAM OBSERVATION
MEASURES ($N = 25$ OBSERVERS)

| Instrument | % Exact Agreement | | % Close Agreement | |
	Range for Individual Items	Average	Range for Individual Items	Average
Arnett	75.0–100	95.3	95.0–100	99.8
ECERS	61.9–100	90.5	66.7–100	95.5
PIP	66.7–100	89.5	90.5–100	98.6

and then asked to independently complete ratings on an assigned program site. The percentages of exact and of close agreement for each item were then calculated across observers and averaged for the instrument as a whole. Table 29 presents the inter-observer reliabilities for the three observational measures: Arnett, ECERS, and PIP. The average reliability for each measure was quite high, ranging from 89.5 to 95.3 for exact agreement and from 95.5 to 99.8 for close agreement.

Data collection schedule   Program observation data were collected during the spring and early summer of 1991. Observers contacted teachers directly to schedule the observation visits. Because the project had been presented to them as a general study of inservice training and classroom practices, the observers did not know whether each program they visited belonged to the High/Scope or to the comparison group. They observed each program for a half day, completing their ratings on all three instruments simultaneously, based on this observation period.

Data Analysis

Observational data were analyzed using t tests to compare program quality in High/Scope versus comparison settings. Group comparisons were made on the items, subscales, and total scores for each measure. Also, after an overall index of program quality was derived by summing all items across the three observational instruments, the High/Scope and comparison groups were compared on this index. In addition to making the above group-comparisons, we used Pearson correlation coefficients and multiple regressions to investigate the more general relationship between background factors (teacher education and experience, inservice training, and agency environment) and program quality. Subsequent analyses (see Chapter 7) looked at the impact of all these factors on children's development. Results are reported as significant at $p < .05$, two-tailed. In addition, results that are significant at $.05 < p < .10$ are reported as trends when they are corroborated by two or more findings on different measures.

Table 30

GROUP COMPARISONS ON THE ARNETT GLOBAL RATING SCALE

Variable	High/Scope (N = 244)		Comparison (N = 122)		
	Mean	SD	Mean	SD	p
Positively worded items[a]					
1. Speaks warmly to the children	3.4	0.7	3.3	0.8	—
3. Listens attentively when children speak	3.4	0.7	3.3	0.7	—
5. Excited about teaching	2.9	0.8	3.0	0.8	—
7. Enjoys the children	3.2	0.8	3.3	0.8	—
8. Explains reasons for rules	2.6	0.9	2.5	0.9	—
9. Encourages children to try new experiences	2.7	0.8	**2.9**	0.9	(.009)
12. Enthusiastic about children's activities	2.9	0.8	2.9	1.0	—
15. Positive attention to individual children	3.2	0.8	3.1	0.8	—
19. Talks on level children can understand	3.8	0.4	3.8	0.4	—
21. Exercises firmness when necessary	**2.8**	0.6	2.6	0.6	.010
22. Encourages prosocial behavior	2.9	0.8	2.8	0.8	—
24. Positive physical contact	2.7	0.9	2.8	0.9	—
25. Interested in children's activities	3.1	0.8	3.0	0.8	—
27. Sincere in tone and manner	3.6	0.7	3.5	0.6	—
28. Supervises children closely	**2.8**	0.6	2.7	0.6	.078
30. Talks to children at eye level	3.2	0.8	3.3	0.8	—

Results

Arnett Global Rating Scale (Arnett) Findings

Table 30 presents the mean ratings and standard deviations of the High/
Scope and comparison programs on the Arnett Global Rating Scale, and the
significance levels of the *t* tests comparing the two groups.

Ratings for the sample as a whole   In general, programs in the sample were
rated toward the upper end of the Arnett index of teacher style and sensitivity to children's needs. Over 61 percent of the 31 items were rated 3 or
above on a 4-point scale, and the mean rating for the sample as a whole was
3.1.[12] The picture that emerged was one of a warm and supportive environment where teachers were accepting toward children and engaged them on

---

[12]No comparable mean Arnett rating was reported in the NCCSS, and therefore the ToT
sample cannot be compared on this measure with another national sample.

Table 30 (continued)

GROUP COMPARISONS ON THE ARNETT GLOBAL RATING SCALE

Variable	High/Scope (N = 244)		Comparison (N = 122)		
	Mean	SD	Mean	SD	p
Negatively-worded items[b]					
2. Critical of the children	3.8	0.5	3.8	0.4	—
4. Places high value on obedience	3.0	0.9	2.9	0.8	—
6. Distant or detached from children	3.7	0.6	3.6	0.7	—
10. Exercises control over children	2.7	0.7	2.6	0.6	—
11. Speaks with irritation or hostility	3.8	0.5	3.7	0.6	—
13. Threatens children	3.9	0.4	3.9	0.3	—
14. Spends time in nonchild activities	3.5	0.7	3.5	0.7	—
16. Negative physical contact	3.8	0.4	3.9	0.4	—
17. Reprimands children	2.4	0.8	2.5	0.7	—
18. Routine or mechanized teaching style	3.7	0.6	3.6	0.6	—
20. Punishes without explanation	1.4	0.8	1.3	0.7	—
23. Finds fault easily with children	3.8	0.5	3.9	0.4	—
26. Prohibits many activities	3.6	0.7	3.5	0.7	—
29. Unrealistically expects self-control	2.2	0.7	**2.4**	0.7	(.020)
31. Harsh when scolding children	3.9	0.5	3.9	0.4	—
ARNETT Total: Mean of 31 ARNETT items[c]	3.1	0.2	3.1	0.2	—

[a]Positively worded items are scored 1 (not at all) to 4 (very much). Higher scores are always better.

[b]Negatively worded items are scored 1 (very much) to 4 (not at all). Higher scores are always better.

[c]Analysis of the total score was based on complete cases only. Sample sizes were N = 239 for High/Scope and N = 119 for the comparison group. There were no significant differences between complete versus missing cases by group on agency background characteristics.

their own level. Rather than being involved with paperwork or housekeeping chores around the room, staff were involved with the children and their activities. The only area where scores tended to be low was in regard to discipline; teachers generally appeared to reprimand children without explanations. Nevertheless, punishments were not harsh, and they were not undertaken with visible irritation directed toward the children. On the contrary, a positive atmosphere prevailed.

Group comparisons Mean differences between the High/Scope and comparison groups on the 31 Arnett items and the total score were generally small. Three comparisons reached significance at $p < .05$. Of these three differences, one favored High/Scope, and two favored the comparison group. High/Scope teachers exercised firmness when necessary but were

Table 31

GROUP COMPARISONS ON THE EARLY CHILDHOOD
ENVIRONMENT RATING SCALE (ECERS)

Variable	High/Scope (N = 244)		Comparison (N = 122)		
	Mean	SD	Mean	SD	p
Items[a]					
1. Greeting/departing	5.8	1.5	**6.2**	1.3	(.043)
2. Meals/snacks	**5.2**	1.2	5.0	1.4	.077
3. Diapering/toileting	5.4	1.4	5.4	1.4	—
4. Personal grooming (independence)	**4.6**	1.3	4.4	1.2	.049
5. Routine care (individual materials)	**6.5**	1.0	6.3	1.2	.031
6. Learning activities (materials)	5.0	1.4	4.8	1.4	—
7. Relaxation and comfort	4.6	1.7	4.9	1.6	—
8. Room arrangement (organized centers)	**5.9**	1.2	5.5	1.3	.001
9. Child related display	4.7	1.4	4.5	1.5	—
10. Understanding language (receptive)	5.4	1.3	5.6	1.3	—
11. Using language (expressive)	5.5	1.3	5.4	1.4	—
12. Using learning concepts (reasoning)	5.2	1.3	5.1	1.4	—
13. Informal use of language	5.6	1.3	5.4	1.6	—
14. Perceptual/fine-motor activities	5.9	1.2	5.9	1.2	—
15. Supervision of fine-motor activities	5.4	1.2	5.5	1.2	—
16. Space for gross-motor activities	5.3	1.6	**5.8**	1.3	(.004)
17. Gross-motor equipment	4.7	1.6	**5.4**	1.3	(.000)
18. Scheduled time for gross-motor	5.5	1.3	**5.9**	1.0	(.003)
19. Supervision of gross-motor activities	5.6	0.9	5.5	1.1	—
20. Art	5.3	1.6	5.3	1.7	—
21. Music/movement	5.8	1.1	**6.0**	1.0	(.056)
22. Blocks	**6.0**	1.3	5.2	1.6	.000
23. Sand/water	4.9	1.5	4.9	1.7	—
24. Dramatic play	4.2	1.3	4.1	1.3	—
25. Schedule (flexibility)	5.8	1.1	5.7	1.1	—
26. Supervision of creative activities	6.0	1.0	6.0	1.1	—
27. Space to be alone	4.0	1.5	4.0	1.4	—
28. Free play (free choice)	5.7	1.2	5.6	1.5	—
29. Group time (balance of small & large)	**5.9**	1.2	5.6	1.5	.028
30. Cultural awareness	**3.4**	1.6	2.9	1.3	.000
31. Tone (quality of interaction)	5.6	1.2	5.7	1.2	—
32. Provisions for exceptional children	5.2	2.0	5.3	1.6	—

Table 31 (continued)

GROUP COMPARISONS ON THE EARLY CHILDHOOD
ENVIRONMENT RATING SCALE (ECERS)

	High/Scope (N = 244)		Comparison (N = 122)		
Variable	Mean	SD	Mean	SD	p
Subscales and total[b]					
ECERS Personal Care: Mean of items 1–4	5.3	0.9	5.2	0.8	—
ECERS Furnishings: Mean of items 5–9	**5.4**	0.9	5.2	0.9	.055
ECERS Language: Mean of items 10–13	5.5	1.1	5.4	1.2	—
ECERS Motor: Mean of items 14–19	5.5	0.9	5.7	0.8	—
ECERS Creativity: Mean of items 20–26	5.4	0.9	5.3	0.9	—
ECERS Social: Mean of items 27–32	4.9	0.9	4.8	1.0	—
ECERS Total: Mean of 32 items	5.3	0.7	5.2	0.8	—

[a]ECERS items are scored 1 (inadequate) to 7 (excellent).

[b]Analyses of subscale and total scores were based on complete cases only. Sample sizes were N = 237 to 243 for High/Scope and N = 118 to 121 for the comparison group. There were no significant differences between complete versus missing cases by group on agency background characteristics.

more likely than comparison teachers to hold unrealistic expectations for children's self-control. This finding may reflect a zealousness regarding the curriculum's emphasis on children being responsible for their own activities. The other result favoring the comparison group—teachers more often encouraging children to try new experiences—has no potential explanation in the curriculum. In the absence of any supporting data or consistent pattern, it is perhaps wisest not to read too much into these program differences. Given the high quality of the comparison programs in general, it is statistically probable that they would emerge better on one or two of the variables examined.

Early Childhood Environment Rating Scale (ECERS) Findings

Table 31 presents the mean ratings and standard deviations of the High/Scope and comparison programs on the Early Childhood Environment Rating Scale, and the significance levels of the *t* tests comparing the two groups.

Ratings for the sample as a whole   The ECERS ratings also painted a positive portrait of the early childhood programs in the ToT Evaluation sample. Of the 32 items rated on 7-point scales, 72 percent were rated 5 or higher. The mean rating across all programs and items was 5.3 (above "good"). To put this score in context, we can compare it with the mean ECERS rating in the NCCSS sample, which was 3.6 (above "adequate"). This difference in ratings further confirmed our characterization of the ToT sample as relatively high-quality programs.

Average ratings indicated that materials and equipment were appropriate to meet children's personal and educational needs, that the learning environment was varied and stimulating, and that the quality of adult-child interaction was generally positive. Although the overall image was positive, there was still substantial variability both within and across programs. The ECERS has sometimes been criticized for the uniformity of the ratings it produces. Yet, in this study, mean item ratings ranged from 2.9 to 6.5, and most standard deviations were between 1.0 and 1.5. Furthermore, certain program areas (with means below 4.5) emerged as less developed than others (examples are allocation of space for children to play alone, provisions for dramatic play, and promotion of cultural awareness). On balance, however, the programs in this study emerged as well-equipped and well-organized environments in which young children could happily and productively spend their time.

Group comparisons   Group differences on the ECERS were both numerous and meaningful. Nearly a third (10) of the 32 items contrasted produced significant findings at $p < .05$, with 6 favoring High/Scope and 4 favoring comparison programs. High/Scope settings were stronger in the physical organization and arrangement of their programs. Materials promoted independence and self-care among the children. The daily schedule achieved an appropriate developmental balance between large- and small-group activities. And the variety of both materials and activities promoted greater cultural awareness in High/Scope than in comparison settings.

The one dimension on which comparison programs were consistently better than High/Scope programs was in providing for children's large-motor needs. Comparison programs allocated more space, equipment, and time to motor development. Moreover, both the activities and the equipment were rated as varied and developmentally appropriate. One explanation for this difference, according to High/Scope consultants, is that High/Scope advocates taking large-motor equipment out of the classroom to free space for work-time projects, group activities, and an expanded music and movement curriculum. Restricting gross-motor equipment to outdoor areas also serves to minimize boisterous and undirected activity inside the work setting. But unlike early childhood settings where the exercise of large muscles may mean aimless running around, the comparison programs in this study promoted gross-motor skills in the context of other areas of development, such as building and dramatic play. These results suggest that the High/Scope Curriculum could profitably reexamine its position on the placement and use of gross-motor equipment within the early childhood classroom. The comparison programs demonstrate that a greater emphasis on large-motor development can be successfully integrated with a simultaneous emphasis on other developmental skills.

Program Implementation Profile (PIP) Findings

Table 32 on page 122 presents the mean ratings and standard deviations of the High/Scope and comparison programs on the Program Implementation

Profile, and it gives the significance levels of the *t* tests comparing the two groups.

Ratings for the sample as a whole   As with the other two observation measures, the PIP documented the overall high quality of the programs in the ToT Evaluation sample. Half of the mean item ratings were 4.0 or better on a 5-point scale; the mean rating across all programs and items was 3.8. The picture that emerged with the PIP was consistent with that which emerged with the ECERS, i.e., a picture of early childhood programs promoting children's development in well-equipped, carefully supervised, and emotionally supportive environments.

Fidelity to the High/Scope Curriculum   The PIP was the most curriculum-specific of the three observational measures and was therefore useful in assessing the level of High/Scope implementation per se. A central concern of this evaluation was whether the ToT dissemination model worked. Did the transmission from High/Scope consultant to agency trainer to classroom teacher produce a recognizable High/Scope program? The answer was a strong "yes." The mean rating for High/Scope sites across all 24 PIP items was 4.02 out of 5; only two items had mean ratings below 3.

Group comparisons   It was expected, but nevertheless rewarding, to also find a large number of significant differences between the High/Scope and comparison programs. Out of 24 item comparisons, 12 reached significance, and 3 approached significance; all but one of these differences favored High/Scope. The single item that was rated higher for comparison programs—the provision of large-motor equipment—was consistent with the ECERS rating of this area. On all three PIP subscales and the total PIP score, High/Scope programs scored significantly higher than did comparison programs. High/Scope was stronger overall on the physical environment, the activities composing the daily routine, and the content of interactions between adults and children. These findings were even more salient in light of the fact that the ratings were completed by non-High/Scope observers. As noted above, the evaluators deliberately recruited observers who were not familiar with the High/Scope Curriculum and training methods. The fact that such neutral observers nevertheless rated High/Scope programs significantly higher than comparisons on these dimensions of quality makes the differences even more credible.

Consistent with the ECERS, but with greater specificity, the PIP documented that High/Scope programs structured the physical environment to promote child-initiated activities. Organized and labeled activity areas contained materials that were easily accessible to children. A hallmark of the curriculum—the sequence whereby children planned, carried out, and reviewed their chosen activities—was the clearest differentiation between High/Scope and comparison programs. In the High/Scope programs, children were encouraged to make choices, articulate their plans, work with the tools at their disposal, and reflect on their actions and experiences.

The PIP ratings were also consistent with anecdotal evidence from our process analysis and with quantitative data from the independent UK evaluation. Findings in all three cases indicated that teachers were strongest in implementing the room arrangement and daily routine features of the

Table 32

GROUP COMPARISONS ON THE PROGRAM
IMPLEMENTATION PROFILE (PIP)

Variable	High/Scope (N = 244)		Comparison (N = 122)		
	Mean	SD	Mean	SD	p
Items[a]					
1. Room divided into activity areas	**4.6**	0.7	4.2	0.8	.000
2. Adequate work space in each area	**4.7**	0.6	4.5	0.7	.014
3. Room is safe and well maintained	4.8	0.7	4.8	0.5	—
4. Materials are arranged and labeled	**4.1**	1.0	3.0	1.2	.000
5. Enough materials in each area	**4.6**	0.7	4.4	0.9	.019
6. Real household and work objects available	**3.8**	1.1	3.6	1.1	.099
7. Materials are accessible to children	**4.6**	0.7	4.4	0.8	.011
8. Equipment for exercising large muscles	3.9	1.3	**4.3**	1.0	(.000)
9. Materials promote awareness of differences	**2.5**	1.3	2.0	1.1	.000
10. Variety of materials for learning	4.2	0.8	4.1	0.9	—
11. Adults implement consistent daily routine	**4.2**	0.6	4.0	0.8	.008
12. Adults encourage children to plan	**3.8**	1.0	2.4	1.3	.000
13. Adults encourage children to review	**3.4**	1.4	1.9	1.1	.000
14. Daily routine balances plan/do/review	**3.8**	1.2	2.4	0.9	.000
15. Balance of large- & small-group activities	4.6	0.8	4.5	0.9	—
16. Opportunities for children to initiate	4.3	0.7	4.2	0.8	—
17. Adults observe/question/extend	**4.3**	0.8	4.1	1.0	.020
18. Adults participate in children's play	**3.8**	1.2	3.5	1.3	.061
19. Adults balance child vs. adult talk	**4.4**	0.8	4.2	0.8	.051
20. Adults encourage fun with language	2.7	1.3	2.5	1.3	—
21. Adults encourage indep. problem-solving	4.0	1.0	3.9	1.0	—
22. Adults encourage coop. among children	3.7	0.8	3.6	0.9	—
23. Adults maintain reasonable limits	3.8	0.9	4.0	1.0	—
24. Adults maintain awareness of whole room	3.9	0.8	3.9	0.9	—
Subscales and total[b]					
PIP Physical Environment: Mean of items 1–10	**4.2**	0.5	3.9	0.6	.000
PIP Daily Routine: Mean of items 11–16	**4.0**	0.7	3.2	0.7	.000
PIP Adult-Child Interaction: Mean of items 17–24	**3.8**	0.7	3.7	0.8	.031
PIP Total: Mean of 24 PIP items	**4.0**	0.5	3.6	0.6	.000

[a]PIP items are scored 1 (low) to 5 (high).

[b]Analyses of subscale and total scores were based on complete cases only. Sample sizes were
N = 240 to 241 for High/Scope and N = 118 to 120 for the comparison group. There were no
significant differences between complete versus missing cases by group on agency
background characteristics.

High/Scope Curriculum. Moreover, the PIP demonstrated that High/Scope adults were also more likely to use a variety of successful communication strategies throughout the daily routine. High/Scope teachers extended children's play by exercising greater observational skills, asking more open-ended questions, and encouraging children to describe what they were doing. Again, these results were consistent with the program observations conducted by the UK evaluation team. They concluded that the plan-do-review sequence and adult-child interaction strategies were already "quite well understood" after a year of curriculum implementation and that "most staff understood the basic elements" of the High/Scope program (Moore & Smith, 1987, p. 15).

Program Quality

Even though the comparison sites were clearly good programs, differences favoring High/Scope were sufficient in number and magnitude to result in their better overall quality. As emphasized throughout this and the preceding chapter, the comparison as well as the High/Scope programs were run by highly qualified teachers. Moreover, the assessment battery not only reflected High/Scope's definition of quality but also represented the dimensions generally recognized by the field as constituting developmentally appropriate early childhood practices. The high quality of the comparison group, and the generic character of the instruments, actually made it harder to prove that High/Scope training could make a noticeable difference in program quality.

Yet the differences favoring High/Scope, even when small in magnitude, did constitute a meaningful and significant pattern. High/Scope mean scores were higher than those of the comparison group on 66.7 percent of the program observation variables ($x^2 = 11.65$, $df = 1$, $p = .001$). High/Scope programs were also significantly better than comparison programs on the combined index of program quality. When their overall program quality scores were summed across the three observational measures, the High/Scope mean was 339, and the comparison mean, 323 ($p = .025$).[13]

To say that High/Scope programs were better reflects a particular viewpoint of what defines program quality. In this case, we are talking about an environment that not only is well equipped but also organizes, labels, and locates materials in a way that promotes independent access and use by children. We mean that more than having a predictable schedule, the day must regularly give children opportunities to make choices and plans, to carry out activities that reflect their individual interests, and to review their experiences in ways that further reasoning abilities. Finally, "better" is the difference between adults who nurture and adults who not only nurture but also approach activities from the child's intellectual perspective. Better program quality means that adults use observation to assess children's developmental levels and that they use communication to extend children's learning opportunities and language skills.

---

[13]The potential range of program quality scores (the sum of the scores on all 87 items) was 87 (low) to 468 (high).

Agency Factors Affecting Program Quality

Table 33 presents the correlations between various indicators of organizational climate and program quality. The relationships, although generally weak, were consistent with the expectation that the quality of the adult's work environment would affect the quality of the program environment.

- *Salary and benefits.* Program quality was significantly related to higher salaries and better benefit options. This result was consistent with the NCCSS finding that wages were the measure of the adult's work environment that best predicted the child development environment. It is possible that higher monetary rewards attract and retain better teachers or that better teachers are rewarded with higher pay and expanded benefits.

- *Job satisfaction.* The number of job frustrations cited by teachers was negatively associated with program quality. As above, the direction of influence may go either way. Program constraints may frustrate teachers, or poor teachers may create unsatisfactory working situations. The number of job rewards cited by teachers was unrelated to program quality.

- *Administrative support.* The degree of administrative support was significantly associated with program quality. Teachers implemented better programs when they felt that the agency provided for their operational and professional needs.

Teacher Factors Affecting Program Quality

General versus specific education   One focus of current debate is the relative importance of general education versus specific coursework in the

Table 33

ORGANIZATIONAL CLIMATE IN RELATION TO PROGRAM
QUALITY, TOTAL SAMPLE (N = 344 TO 353)

	Correlation With Program Quality Measures			
Agency Variable	Arnett Total	ECERS Total	PIP Total	Program Quality Total
Salary	.11	.03	.13*	.10
Benefits	.10	.03	.10*	.03
Job frustrations	-.18**	-.10	.00	-.07
Job rewards	.06	.05	.04	.00
Administrative support	.16*	.07	.11*	.11*

Note. Analyses were based on complete cases only. A maximum of 22 out of 366 cases were lost, 8 to 12 from the High/Scope sample and 7 to 10 from the comparison sample. There were no significant differences between complete versus missing cases on program characteristics.

*p < .05. **p < .01.

preparation of early childhood teachers. Table 34 contrasts the program quality of teachers with versus without 4-year college degrees. It also contrasts the program quality of those with versus without early childhood degrees or credentials.

- Teachers with college degrees implemented better quality programs than did teachers without degrees; likewise, teachers with early childhood degrees or credentials implemented better quality programs than did teachers without such preparation.

- Overall, a college degree differentiated program quality more than an early childhood degree or credential did. There were 8 significant differences attributable to the former, compared with 5 attributable to the latter.

- Programs in which teachers had college degrees or credentials did significantly better on subscales or total scores of all three quality measures. Teachers with college degrees implemented programs that provided better physical, socioemotional, and cognitive environments for young children than did teachers without college degrees.

- Programs in which teachers had early childhood degrees did better on several scales, particularly on those assessing the physical environment. Teachers with an early childhood degree were better than teachers without this degree at providing materials for children to develop creative and social skills.

Education versus training versus experience   Another question in the early childhood field concerns the relative contributions of teachers' formal education, inservice training, and experience to program quality. Table 35 presents the correlations between these background variables and each of the program quality measures individually. Table 36 presents the results of regression equations investigating the relative contributions of background factors, as well as the relative contribution of group (High/Scope versus comparison), to overall program quality.

As Table 35 shows, formal education, inservice training, and teaching experience were *all* highly significant predictors of program quality. Other studies cited earlier (e.g., Ruopp, 1979; Whitebook et al., 1989) found that education and early childhood training, but not experience, were determinants of good caregiving. One explanation for the current finding may lie in the generally high quality of the programs observed in this study. Perhaps experience, when obtained in the context of a good program environment, *does* provide teachers with the role models and support they need to develop appropriate practices. Experience in a poor learning environment cannot serve as a route to professional development.

This interpretation connecting training with experience is supported by the significant effect of group in the regression equations (Table 36). Considering inservice training, on the one hand, we find that in High/Scope programs, where inservice training was more uniform, such training was not a significant predictor of program quality; yet in comparison programs, it was a very strong positive predictor of program quality. Experience, on the other hand, though significantly affecting quality in both groups, had

Table 34

THE RELATIONSHIP OF COLLEGE DEGREE AND EARLY CHILDHOOD PREPARATION TO PROGRAM QUALITY

Program Quality Variable	Degree		No Degree		
	Mean	SD	Mean	SD	p
A. Quality related to college degree versus no college degree					
	(N = 240)		(N = 112)		
Arnett Total	**3.2**	0.4	3.0	0.4	.006
ECERS Personal Care	5.3	0.9	5.2	0.9	—
ECERS Furnishings	**5.4**	0.9	5.0	0.8	.000
ECERS Language	**5.6**	1.1	5.1	1.2	.001
ECERS Motor	**5.7**	0.8	5.3	0.8	.000
ECERS Creativity	**5.5**	0.9	5.2	0.9	.004
ECERS Social	**5.0**	0.9	4.5	0.9	.000
ECERS Total	**5.3**	0.7	5.0	0.8	.002
PIP Physical Environment	4.1	0.6	4.0	0.6	—
PIP Daily Routine	3.8	0.8	3.7	0.8	—
PIP Adult-Child Interaction	**3.8**	0.7	3.6	0.7	.006
PIP Total	3.9	0.6	3.8	0.6	—
PROGRAM QUALITY Total	**359.4**	43.4	343.4	49.3	.070
B. Quality related to early childhood degree or credential versus no early childhood preparation					
	(N = 256)		(N = 101)		
Arnett Total	5.3	0.4	5.1	0.4	—
ECERS Personal Care	5.3	0.9	5.2	0.9	—
ECERS Furnishings	**5.4**	0.8	5.1	1.0	.011
ECERS Language	5.5	1.1	5.3	1.2	—
ECERS Motor	5.6	0.8	5.5	0.9	—
ECERS Creativity	**5.4**	0.8	5.2	1.0	.022
ECERS Social	**5.0**	0.9	4.7	0.9	.008
ECERS Total	**5.3**	0.7	5.1	0.9	.013
PIP Physical Environment	4.2	0.5	4.0	0.7	.013
PIP Daily Routine	3.8	0.8	3.7	0.8	—
PIP Adult-Child Interaction	3.8	0.7	3.8	0.7	—
PIP Total	3.9	0.6	3.8	0.6	—
PROGRAM QUALITY Total	358.3	43.5	347.8	50.1	—

Note. The Arnett uses a 4-point scale, the ECERS uses a 7-point scale, and the PIP uses a 5-point scale. Program quality scores can range from 87 to 468. Higher scores are always better.

Table 35

TEACHER FACTORS AFFECTING PROGRAM QUALITY,
TOTAL SAMPLE (N = 344 TO 353)

	Correlations With Program Quality Measures			
Teacher Variable	Arnett Total	ECERS Total	PIP Total	Program Quality Total
Education				
Years of formal education	.19**	.20***	.11*	.17*
Experience				
Years of early childhood experience	.15*	.11*	.17**	.10
Inservice training				
Hours of inservice training provided by agency	.21***	.10	.11*	.18*
Sessions with outside presenters	.04	-.05	.01	-.07
Sessions with agency consultant	.09	.01	.12*	.08
Classroom visits	.13*	.07	.05	.09
Curriculum workshops	.09	.10	.06	.16*

Note. Analyses were based on complete cases only. A maximum of 22 out of 366 cases were lost, 8 to 12 from High/Scope and 7 to 10 from the comparison sample. There were no significant differences between complete versus missing cases on program characteristics.

*p < .05. **p < .01. ***p < .001.

a stronger relationship to quality in the High/Scope group. In High/Scope programs, where inservice training was significantly more likely to be both provided and required, teachers obtained their experience in the context of systematic ongoing professional development.

The specific aspects of inservice training associated with program quality were curriculum workshops and classroom visits conducted by in-house consultants (Table 35). As the group comparisons in previous chapters showed, these features are the hallmarks that distinguish High/Scope's adult training methods from other approaches in the field.

Summary of Program Observation Results

Program Comparisons

1. Both High/Scope and comparison settings offered high-quality early childhood programs.

- Both groups provided safe and well-equipped physical environments.

Table 36

GENERAL EDUCATION, EARLY CHILDHOOD
EXPERIENCE, INSERVICE TRAINING, AND GROUP
AS DETERMINANTS OF PROGRAM QUALITY

Predictor Variable	Beta	p
A. Total sample ($N = 344$)		
Years of early childhood experience	.32	.000
Amount of inservice training	.33	.000
Years of education	.44	.000
Group (High/Scope vs. comparison)	.21	.005
Multiple R	.43	.000[a]
B. High/Scope sample ($N = 232$)		
Years of early childhood experience	.36	.000
Amount of inservice training	.12	n.s.
Years of education	.39	.000
Multiple R	.39	.006[b]
C. Comparison sample ($N = 112$)		
Years of early childhood experience	.29	.005
Amount of inservice training	.67	.000
Years of education	.20	.050
Multiple R	.65	.000[c]

[a]$F = 9.63, DF = 3.$ [b]$F = 8.48, DF = 3.$ [c]$F = 20.10, DF = 3.$

■ Both groups had nurturing adults who were sensitive to children's needs.

2. High/Scope programs were better than comparison programs in organizing the physical environment, encouraging independent thought and action, and using adult-child interaction to promote reasoning and language skills.

■ High/Scope programs were better than comparison programs at organizing and labeling their rooms and guaranteeing the accessibility of materials in order to promote children's greater independence, self-care, initiative, and multicultural awareness.

■ High/Scope programs were better than comparison programs in encouraging children to choose activities based on their interests, to carry out plans in accordance with their developmental levels, and to reflect on their actions and experiences through representation and communication.

■ High/Scope teachers were better than comparison teachers at extending children's play through the use of observations and open-ended questions.

3. Comparison programs were better than High/Scope programs in supporting children's gross-motor development.

- Comparison programs provided more equipment, space, and time for large-muscle activities than did High/Scope programs.

- Comparison programs used gross-motor equipment and activities in the context of developing other skills, such as building and dramatic play.

Factors Affecting Program Quality

4. Organizational climate was significantly associated with the level of program quality.

- Program quality was significantly related to higher salaries and better benefit options.

- The number of job frustrations cited by teachers was negatively associated with program quality.

- The degree of administrative support was significantly associated with program quality. Teachers implemented better programs when they felt that the agency provided for their operational and professional needs.

5. Teachers with college degrees and teachers with early childhood preparation implemented better quality programs than did teachers without such background.

- Overall, a college degree differentiated program quality more than did an early childhood degree.

- Teachers with college degrees implemented programs that provided better physical, socioemotional, and cognitive environments for young children than did teachers without college degrees.

- Teachers with early childhood degrees or credentials were better than teachers without this preparation at providing materials for children to develop creative and social skills.

6. Formal education, inservice training, and teaching experience were all highly significant positive predictors of program quality.

- Other studies have found that teaching experience by itself does not result in good caregiving. The current results suggest that teaching experience obtained in the context of a good program environment can provide the role models and support needed for professional development.

- The types of inservice training associated with program quality were curriculum workshops and classroom visits conducted by in-house consultants.

VII The Child Study

The Child Study completed the evaluation chain by assessing 97 children in High/Scope programs and 103 children in non-High/Scope, comparison, sites. Children in High/Scope programs were rated significantly higher than those in comparison programs on initiative, social relations, music and movement, and overall development. They also tended to have higher scores on cognitive development. Comparison children did not outscore High/Scope children on any measures. For the sample as a whole, teaching experience, inservice training, and program quality, but not teachers' formal education, were significant positive predictors of child outcomes. Children's access to diverse materials and their opportunities for planning and recall were the two dimensions of program quality most strongly and consistently related to child development. Children's language and representational skills were the two areas of development most affected by program quality.

Purpose

The Child Study looked at the final link in the dissemination chain—the transmission from teacher to child. In focusing on the impact of program practices on the development of young children, this phase of the research served three important purposes: First, it enabled High/Scope to document the effectiveness of its curriculum as compared with other early childhood program practices. Although High/Scope has been engaged in extensive longitudinal follow-up of those adults who, as children, attended its preschool programs in 1962–65, before this ToT Evaluation the Foundation had no systematic current data on children in its programs. Second, along with the promotion of its own curriculum, High/Scope has always been concerned with promoting high-quality early childhood programs in general. The evaluation thus provided an opportunity to investigate the relationship between program quality—defined in terms of developmental appropriateness—and children's development. Finally, the study allowed us to examine the relative contributions of several factors (teacher education and experience, inservice training, organizational climate, and program quality) to the growth of young children.

Procedures

The Sample

The sample of 200 children was drawn entirely from Michigan to permit detailed assessment within time and budget limitations. Because the child assessment procedures required 3 days of observation in each setting, the evaluators restricted the child sample to programs within a 2-hour drive of the Foundation. The variety of Michigan sites, however, was sufficient to ensure that the children were representative of the diversity in the sample as a whole. Michigan programs selected for the child sample were located in urban and rural settings, operated within a wide range of agencies, and served children across a broad spectrum of ethnic and socioeconomic backgrounds.[14]

Approximately 8 children were assessed in each of 13 High/Scope and 13 comparison programs. Teachers provided the names of children according to random selection procedures developed by the researchers. The names were chosen by applying rules of numerical order to alphabetized lists. Selection procedures also insured that children fell within the age-range appropriate for the assessment measures (2 to 6 years), that there was an equal mix of boys and girls, and that children who were frequently absent would not be included, to minimize the risk of missing data.

The resulting sample was composed of 200 children, approximately half High/Scope (48.5 percent) and half comparison (51.5 percent), from 15 agencies operating 21 sites. Children were observed in a total of 26 different program settings. Table 37 describes the child sample according to agency type and background characteristics for the High/Scope and comparison groups. The two groups were closely matched on demographic variables. Overall, nearly half came from Head Start programs, a fifth from public schools, and over a third from other nonprofit agencies. Males and females were equally represented in the total sample and in each group. The mean age of the children in each group was just over 4 years. Seven of the 15 agencies used to draw the sample served predominantly minority or mixed populations. Accordingly, over half of the child sample came from African American, Hispanic, or other minority groups. On average, parents in each group had completed high school and attended 1 to 2 years of college. Occupational levels for mothers and fathers in the two groups were also equivalent.

Instrumentation

Two standardized instruments were used in the Child Study, an observational measure and a screening test:

The High/Scope Child Observation Record (COR) for Ages 2½–6   The COR is an observational tool for looking at children in their natural program setting and rating them along a variety of behavioral dimensions. The measure was originally devised to observe children engaging in the High/Scope key experiences. It was later developed as a generic instrument that could be used regardless of a program's curriculum model. The reliability and validity of this generic version of the COR were documented in a study of approximately 500 children and 128 Head Start teaching staff in southeastern Michigan (Schweinhart, McNair, Barnes, & Larner, 1991). The COR consists of 30 items, each with a 5-point rating scale, for assessing child-

---

[14]No children in the sample came from for-profit programs. Because there were no for-profit High/Scope programs within a reasonable geographical radius, no for-profit comparison programs were observed either. Since for-profits accounted for the smallest proportion (12 percent) of the total study population, it was felt that their absence would not unduly skew the results of the Child Study.

Table 37

BACKGROUND CHARACTERISTICS OF THE CHILD SAMPLE

Variable	High/Scope (N = 97)	Comparison (N = 103)
Agency type		
Head Start	44%	47%
Public school	24%	15%
Nonprofit	32%	39%
For-profit	0%	0%
Sex of children		
Male	45%	48%
Female	55%	52%
Age of children		
Mean	4.4 yr	4.3 yr
Distribution		
2-year-olds	3%	4%
3-year-olds	9%	11%
4-year-olds	48%	46%
5-year-olds	38%	35%
6-year-olds	2%	4%
Ethnicity		
White	41%	45%
African American	31%	32%
Hispanic	9%	2%
Native American	2%	0%
Middle Eastern	2%	5%
Other	9%	14%
Parent's completed education		
Father (mean)	13.7 yr	13.6 yr
Mother (mean)	13.5 yr	13.8 yr
Parent's median occupational level[a]		
Father	Laborer	Laborer
Mother	Service worker	Service worker

[a]Bureau of Labor Statistics Codes

initiated behaviors in six areas of development: initiative, social relations, creative representation, language and literacy, logic and mathematics, and music and movement. In addition to scores for individual items and subscales, a COR total score was derived from the mean rating across all 30 COR items.

The Developmental Indicators for the Assessment of Learning—Revised (DIAL-R)   The DIAL-R is a broad screening tool for assessing the behavior of children aged 2 to 6 in three areas: motor, concepts, and language. It was normed on a national sample of 2,500 children, stratified by age, ethnicity, and sex. The DIAL-R can be administered in a short span of time (generally under 30 minutes), and assessors require training but not certification to administer the measure. Its developers note that the instrument possesses ecological validity, i.e., the testing situation is set up using activity centers typically found in early childhood programs, and the 24 items are game-like in nature. Although the DIAL-R was designed as a screening instrument, the scaled scores are also appropriate for use in developmental comparisons or program evaluations. The ToT Evaluation used the DIAL-R for these latter purposes. In addition to scores for individual items and subscales, a DIAL-R total score was derived from the mean scores across all 24 DIAL-R items.

The researchers had some reservations about administering a screening test—questions about the appropriateness of screening tests for use with children and about their validity as developmental indicators. Their decision to use a screening test, and specifically the DIAL-R, was based on several factors:

Supplementary measurement. In investigating the relationship between program quality and child outcomes, High/Scope acknowledged the need to address that portion of the audience wanting a widely recognized test to supplement the observational data.

Age of assessment. The DIAL-R was chosen because it satisfied our requirement for a measure that could be used with children who were 2 to 6 years of age; several equally valid measures did not go below age 3 or above age 5.

Psychometric properties. Recent studies (Mardell-Czudnowski & Goldenberg, 1990) indicated that the DIAL-R had acceptable psychometric properties. In addition to its construct and concurrent validity, the measure appeared to be a reasonable predictor of subsequent academic performance. In an evaluation of High/Scope preschool classrooms, Frede and Barnett (1992) found that the DIAL-R significantly predicted scores on a measure of school readiness in kindergarten and first grade.

The effectiveness of the High/Scope Preschool Curriculum in preparing children for school is a legitimate research question. Because the COR has not been in existence long enough to compile predictive data, the researchers decided that using a standardized screening measure such as the DIAL-R would allow the evaluation to begin addressing this question. Correlations between the two instruments, presented in Table 38, indicated that they were complementary measures of young children's development. Their strongest associations (r ranging from .40 to .60 at $p < .001$) were in the traditional academic areas of language and mathematics. Yet each contributed unique items in these domains, while the COR addressed a wider variety of nontraditional developmental issues.

Data Collection

Training   Eight of the 14 Michigan program observers (see Chapter 6) were also trained to administer the child assessments. A member of the research

Table 38

CORRELATION OF ToT CHILD ASSESSMENT MEASURES
FOR TOTAL SAMPLE (N = 139 TO 199)

	DIAL-R			
COR Variables	Motor	Concepts	Language	Total
Initiative	.12*	.17**	.08	.17**
Social Relations	.32***	.35**	.35***	.36***
Creative Representation	.26***	.26***	.20**	.28***
Language & Literacy	.40***	.47***	.41***	.46***
Logic & Mathematics	.55***	.57***	.46***	.60***
Music & Movement	.31***	.25***	.28***	.31***
COR Total	.47***	.49***	.42***	.51***

Note. Analyses of subscale and total scores were based on complete cases only. A maximum of 61 out of 200 cases were lost, 0 to 29 from High/Scope and 1 to 32 from the comparison group. There were no significant differences between complete versus missing cases by group on demographic characteristics.

* $p < .05$. ** $p < .01$. *** $p < .001$.

team conducted the training, observing practice sessions and computing inter-observer reliability. The observers' COR ratings were compared with those of the trainer, to assess both exact agreement and close agreement (within one scale point). DIAL-R operators were trained using the procedures described in the DIAL-R manual, which specifies a criterion of 100 percent agreement on the written test and a minimum of 90 percent agreement on the performance test.

Inter-observer reliability   Table 39 presents inter-observer reliabilities on the two child assessments (defined as the percentage obtained by dividing the number of agreements by the total number of agreements plus disagreements). Average reliability on the COR was quite high, 92.8 percent for exact agreement and 97.8 percent for close agreement (within one scoring level) across all 30 items. According to the standards for exact agreement in the DIAL-R manual, reliability on the written test was 100 percent, as required, while that for the performance test averaged 93.8 percent across the 24 items.

Data collection schedule   Child assessments were collected in the late spring and early summer of 1991. Assessors visited the programs in teams of three. Two members of the team each observed 4 children and completed the COR; the third member administered the DIAL-R to all 8 designated children. Observations in each setting were carried out over 3 half-days as children engaged in their typical program activities. If a child was absent, return visits were scheduled to enable the team to complete its assessment. The 3-day period was chosen to guarantee that observers would get to know each target child well enough to complete all the items on the COR; it also

Table 39

INTER-OBSERVER RELIABILITY ON CHILD ASSESSMENTS
(N = 8 CHILD ASSESSORS)

| | % Exact Agreement | | % Close Agreement | |
Instrument	Range for Individual Items	Average	Range for Individual Items	Average
COR	69.7–100.0	92.8	87.9–100.0	97.8
DIAL-R				
Written	100.0–100.0	100.0	not applicable	
Performance	90.0–100.0	93.8	not applicable	

maximized the chance that all the behaviors of interest would have an opportunity to occur during this span of time. Despite these safeguards, nearly a third of the children could not be rated on one or more of the COR items. Missing data occurred most often on the items making up the logic and mathematics subscale. As noted in the analyses below, however, there were no significant demographic differences by group between children with complete versus incomplete observational ratings. Missing data did not interfere with the analyses, although the lower N's on the affected subscale and on the total scores made it less likely that differences would reach significance.

Data Analysis

Procedures for analyzing the child data were similar to those used for program data. Children's development in the High/Scope versus comparison programs were compared using t tests. Pearson correlation coefficients explored the relationship between program quality and child outcomes. Results are reported as significant at $p < .05$, two-tailed. In addition, results that are significant at $.05 < p < .10$ are reported as trends when they are corroborated by two or more findings on different measures.

The final step in the analysis used Pearson correlation coefficients to explore the relationship of teacher background, inservice training, and program quality, on the one hand, with children's development, on the other. In doing these analyses, we were faced with the classical dilemma of educational researchers, i.e., whether to use the *individual child* or the *group of children in a program* as the unit of analysis. Because teacher factors and program quality were measured at the program level, the researchers chose to also analyze child data at the program level. Thus the mean score across all children in the same program was used in the correlations. This procedure reduced the sample size from 200 children to 26 programs for the whole group, and to only 13 programs when we examined the High/Scope and comparison groups separately. (Ideally, with more time and money, we would have sampled children from a larger number of programs.) Because it is difficult to obtain significant results with such a small sample, results significant at $p < .10$ are reported, to avoid overlooking meaningful findings that might have reached significance with a larger N.

Results

The Screening Test (DIAL-R) Findings

Table 40 presents the group comparisons on the DIAL-R items, subscales, total score, and behavioral ratings.

Group comparisons on the DIAL-R test   Although children in High/Scope programs had higher mean scores on 83.3 percent of (20 out of 24) DIAL-R items, the difference for only one item was significant, while for two others the differences approached significance. High/Scope children, who scored significantly higher on naming verbs and approached significant differences on naming nouns, appeared to have better language skills than did comparison children. A High/Scope advantage in these skills would be consistent with the curriculum's components of planning and recall. During these periods, children are encouraged to describe their activities and the materials they use during work time. The High/Scope group also tended to outscore the comparison group on the cognitive task of sorting. Children in High/Scope programs would have ample opportunities during work time, cleanup time, and small-group time to engage in classification activities. Subscale and total scores, while again favoring the High/Scope group, were not significantly different.

On the primarily academic tasks of the DIAL-R, therefore, the High/Scope Curriculum did not appear to facilitate children's performance a great deal better than other program models did. Although the trends were consistent with children's learning opportunities in the High/Scope Curriculum, only one difference reached significance. The absence of many significant findings also suggested that the two groups were comparable in the distribution of the kinds of developmental problems that the DIAL-R screens for. Because testing was done at the end of the program year, it was not surprising that the incidence of apparent problems was low in both sample groups.

Group comparisons on behavior ratings during DIAL-R testing   After administering each of the three DIAL-R sections, operators also rated children's behavior on eight dimensions: separation, crying, unwillingness to answer/respond, giving up easily, distractibility, hyperactivity, resistance, and disruptiveness. Analyses indicated that comparison children exhibited significantly more problems during the motor testing and that they also tended toward more problem behavior during the language test. Follow-up analyses indicated that the specific behavior responsible for these differences was *hyperactivity*, i.e., comparison children were rated as hyperactive during testing significantly more often than High/Scope children were.

Table 40

GROUP COMPARISONS ON THE DEVELOPMENTAL INDICATORS
FOR THE ASSESSMENT OF LEARNING—REVISED (DIAL-R)

Variable	High/Scope (N = 97)		Comparison (N = 103)		
	Mean	SD	Mean	SD	p
Items[a]					
1. Catching	2.6	1.3	2.7	1.2	—
2. Jumping	3.3	0.9	3.1	1.1	—
3. Building	2.9	1.0	2.8	1.0	—
4. Touching	3.3	1.4	3.1	1.4	—
5. Cutting	2.5	0.8	2.3	1.1	—
6. Matching	3.1	0.8	2.8	0.9	—
7. Copying	2.2	1.0	2.0	1.2	—
8. Writing	1.3	1.7	1.1	1.7	—
9. Body parts	2.9	1.0	2.7	1.0	—
10. Colors	2.8	0.6	2.8	0.5	—
11. Rote counting	3.2	1.3	3.2	1.3	—
12. Meaningful counting	2.8	1.2	2.6	1.2	—
13. Position	2.6	1.1	2.5	1.1	—
14. Concepts	3.2	0.7	3.1	0.8	—
15. Letters	2.8	1.4	3.0	1.3	—
16. Sorting	**2.3**	1.7	1.9	1.7	.073
17. Speaking and articulating	2.4	0.6	2.4	0.6	—
18. Providing personal data	2.7	1.0	2.6	1.1	—
19. Remembering	3.3	0.9	3.1	0.9	—
20. Naming nouns	**3.6**	0.7	3.4	0.9	.080
21. Naming verbs	**3.7**	0.7	3.4	0.9	.043
22. Classifying foods	2.9	1.3	2.9	1.3	—
23. Problem solving	3.1	1.0	3.1	1.0	—
24. Sentence length	3.6	0.8	3.5	0.9	—
Subscales and total[b]					
DIAL-R Motor: Mean of items 1–8	2.6	0.7	2.5	0.8	—
DIAL-R Concept: Mean of items 9–16	2.8	0.8	2.7	0.8	—
DIAL-R Language: Mean of items 17–24	3.1	0.5	3.0	0.6	—
DIAL-R Total: Mean of 24 items	2.9	0.6	2.8	0.7	—

Table 40 (continued)

GROUP COMPARISONS ON THE DEVELOPMENTAL INDICATORS
FOR THE ASSESSMENT OF LEARNING—REVISED (DIAL-R)

Variable	High/Scope (N = 97)		Comparison (N = 103)		
	Mean	SD	Mean	SD	p
Behavioral problems[c]					
During Motor test	0.1	0.4	**0.2**	0.7	(.051)
During Concept test	0.1	0.6	0.2	0.6	—
During Language test	0.1	0.5	**0.3**	0.7	.081

[a]DIAL-R items are scored 0 (low) to 4 (high).

[b]Analyses of subscale and total scores were based on complete cases only. Sample sizes were N = 93 to 97 for High/Scope and N = 98 to 102 for the comparison group. There were no significant differences between complete versus missing cases by group on demographic characteristics.

[c]Higher scores indicate *more* problems in one or more of the following areas: separation, crying, unwillingness to answer, giving up easily, distractibility, hyperactivity, resistance, and disruptiveness.

The Observational Measure (COR) Findings

Table 41 presents the group comparisons on the COR items, subscales, total score, and general behavioral ratings.

Group comparisons on COR observations The High/Scope group rated significantly higher than comparisons on three of the six COR subscales, approached significance on a fourth, and rated significantly higher on the COR total score. Subscales significantly favoring the High/Scope group were initiative, social relations, and music and movement. The subscale approaching significance was creative representation. Moreover, High/Scope children outscored comparison children on 83.3 percent of (25 out of 30) COR observation items. Two of these differences were significant, and five approached significance. These findings show that the High/Scope ToT dissemination chain successfully held up from Foundation consultants to agency-based trainers to program teachers to young children.

High/Scope children's demonstration of greater initiative and self-confidence was consistent with the goals and approach of the curriculum. They were encouraged to make choices, and the organization of the room and its materials enabled them to act out their plans with a high degree of independence and self-direction. Similarly, the emphasis on recall following these activities would logically lead to enhanced representational abilities. This interpretation is supported by the independent evaluation conducted by the Oxford team in the United Kingdom. Berry and Sylva (1987) found that the vast majority of children could plan (91 percent) and recall (86 percent), often with elaborated detail that provided "clear evidence of internal representation."

Table 41

GROUP COMPARISONS ON THE CHILD OBSERVATION RECORD (COR)

Variable	High/Scope (N = 97)		Comparison (N = 103)		
	Mean	SD	Mean	SD	p
Items[a]					
1. Expressing choices	3.1	0.5	3.1	0.5	—
2. Solving problems	3.5	0.7	3.4	0.8	—
3. Complex play	**3.4**	1.1	3.2	1.0	.057
4. Cooperation	**3.7**	0.8	3.5	0.9	.094
5. Relating to adults	3.9	0.8	3.8	0.7	—
6. Relating to children	**4.2**	0.7	4.0	0.7	.027
7. Making friends	2.7	1.1	2.6	1.0	—
8. Social problem solving	**3.4**	1.2	3.0	1.3	.072
9. Expressing feelings	3.4	1.0	3.3	1.0	—
10. Making and building	3.4	1.0	3.4	1.0	—
11. Drawing and painting	3.1	1.1	2.9	1.1	—
12. Pretending and role play	3.5	1.1	3.3	1.1	—
13. Understanding speech	3.8	0.7	3.9	0.7	—
14. Speaking	3.1	1.0	3.1	1.0	—
15. Interest in reading	3.0	1.1	2.8	1.0	—
16. Knowledge about books	2.5	0.7	2.5	0.9	—
17. Beginning reading	1.9	0.4	2.0	0.4	—
18. Beginning writing	2.7	0.7	2.5	0.7	—
19. Arranging materials	2.2	1.2	2.0	1.2	—
20. Using comparison words	3.1	1.1	3.1	1.0	—
21. Sorting	**2.6**	1.3	2.3	1.2	.095
22. Using *not/some/all*	2.9	0.9	2.9	0.8	—
23. Comparing numbers of objects	2.2	0.8	2.1	0.8	—
24. Counting objects	**3.4**	0.8	3.2	0.9	.095
25. Describing spatial relationships	3.3	1.0	3.5	0.1	—
26. Describing sequence and time	3.4	1.3	3.5	1.5	—
27. Body coordination	4.1	1.0	4.1	1.0	—
28. Manual coordination	3.8	1.1	3.5	1.1	—
29. Imitating movement to a steady beat	**3.6**	1.2	3.1	1.3	.015
30. Following directions in movement	3.3	1.3	3.1	1.1	—
Subscales and total[b]					
COR Initiative: Mean of items 1–4	**3.5**	0.5	3.3	0.5	.005
COR Social Relations: Mean of items 5–9	**3.6**	0.5	3.4	0.6	.010
COR Representation: Mean of items 10–12	**3.4**	0.8	3.2	0.7	.089

Table 41 (continued)

GROUP COMPARISONS ON THE CHILD OBSERVATION RECORD (COR)

Variable	High/Scope (N = 97)		Comparison (N = 103)		
	Mean	SD	Mean	SD	p
COR Language: Mean of items 13–18	2.9	0.4	2.8	0.5	—
COR Logic & Math: Mean of items 19–26	2.9	0.6	2.8	0.6	—
COR Music & Movement: Mean of items 27–30	**3.9**	0.8	3.5	0.7	.005
COR Total: Mean of 30 items	**3.4**	0.4	3.2	0.5	.035
COR observer's general ratings of child[c]					
Distracted/absorbed	3.0	0.6	3.0	0.7	—
Gives up/persistent	3.1	0.5	3.0	0.7	—
Prefers easy/challenging tasks	3.1	0.5	3.1	0.6	—
Distrusts ability/confident	**3.2**	0.6	3.1	0.6	.057
Passive/overactive (3 = normal)	3.0	0.4	**3.1**	0.7	(.090)

[a]COR items are scored 1 (low) to 5 (high).

[b]Analyses of subscale and total scores were based on complete cases only. Sample sizes were $N = 68$ to 82 for the High/Scope group and $N = 71$ to 99 for the comparison group. There were no significant differences between complete versus missing cases by group on demographic characteristics.

[c]Behavior ratings are scored 1 to 5 along each continuum listed.

The significantly higher scores on social relationships were also consistent with the anecdotal reports in the process analysis. Children were encouraged to interact by sharing their ideas at planning and recall time, collaborating on tasks at work time, and helping one another to answer questions and solve problems. Teachers and trainers, observing fewer discipline problems and greater cooperation among children, surmised that the High/Scope approach eliminated the root of many behavioral difficulties, e.g., children's boredom and competition for scarce resources. These impressions were supported by the quantitative data that reached or approached significance. Confirmation of the relationship between the curriculum model and children's behavior also came from the UK study. Berry and Sylva (1987) reported that children involved in High/Scope's plan-do-review sequence were significantly less likely to engage in "boisterous" body games and roughhousing. Periods labeled free time, by contrast, were more likely to have children running about in the kinds of aimless activity that could lead to physical conflicts and would make it harder for teachers to engage children in more productive tasks.

One finding that was initially puzzling were scores favoring music and movement in High/Scope children, despite the earlier findings (of program observers) that comparison programs provided significantly more opportunities for motor development. Closer examination revealed that the significant variables in the program and child observations were measuring different areas of growth. While comparison programs offered more space, equipment, and time for gross-motor development, the High/Scope programs specifically emphasized the music and movement aspects of the curriculum. Thus High/Scope children scored significantly higher on the item "moving to a steady beat." On other indices of motor development, the COR was consistent with the DIAL-R in showing no significant group differences.

Finally, the fact that children in High/Scope programs did significantly better than comparisons on socioemotional rather than on cognitive (math and logic) indicators deserves further discussion. In its incarnation in the early 1960s, the High/Scope program was named the Cognitively Oriented Curriculum. Its emphasis on Piagetian concepts, which pioneered later work in this field, led some advocates of traditional nursery schools to think that the program overlooked noncognitive aspects of growth. Even today, High/Scope is mistakenly seen by some as slighting children's affective and social development. Perhaps what we are now seeing, 30 years later, is the evolution of the early childhood field. Cognitive processes, such as classification and seriation, are now the standard language of early childhood teacher training and program development. The rest of the field may have caught up with those who early on recognized the impact of the program environment on children's intellectual growth. By the same token, the present High/Scope Curriculum states explicitly the potential of cognitive processes for promoting children's affective and interpersonal development, and the curriculum has expanded its focus on socioemotional key experiences. High/Scope emphasizes that the intellectual activities embodied in the plan-do-review sequence hold myriad opportunities for children to exercise their initiative, imagination, and social skills. The Child Study data clearly indicate that this program framework successfully supports young children's affective and interpersonal growth.

Group comparisons on COR general ratings   After observing children for 3 days, COR observers also rated them on five general behavioral dimensions: distracted/absorbed, gives up/persistent, prefers easy/challenging tasks, distrusts ability/confident, and passive/overactive. Analyses on two of these dimensions approached significance. High/Scope children tended to be more confident than comparison children, and comparison children tended to be more overactive than High/Scope children. This latter finding is consistent with the hyperactivity ratings during the DIAL-R testing. Thus, although only some of the comparisons reached significance, there was clearly a pattern of more hyperactivity within the comparison sample. Looking to contrasting curriculum approaches to explain this difference, we can surmise that the High/Scope plan-do-review sequence resulted in greater patience among the children. These behavior ratings by outside observers supported the observations of teachers and trainers in ToT projects, who noted an increase in attention spans when children were able to focus on activities of their own choice.

Direction of Mean Differences on Child Measures

As just noted, 83 percent of the 24 DIAL-R scores and 83 percent of the 30 COR ratings favored children in the High/Scope group over those in the comparison group (x^2 = 44.09, df = 1, p = .001). Although just under one fifth (19 percent) of these mean differences reached significance, their consistency did suggest a pattern of greater social, cognitive, and language development within the High/Scope group. It is further noteworthy that there were no significant differences favoring children in the comparison group.

The Relationship of Program Quality to Child Measures

Program quality and the DIAL-R   Table 42 presents the correlations between program observation measures and children's scores on the DIAL-R for the total sample (N = 26 programs) and for each group separately (N = 13 programs). For the total sample, the overall index of program quality was positively and significantly related to the DIAL-R total score (r = .32, p < .05). This relationship was even higher in the comparison group (r = .45, p < .10), and also positive though not significant in the High/Scope group (r = .28). These findings were consistent with the hypothesis that program quality would play a role in children's development. Given measurement error and other competing influences on a young child's growth (e.g., sociodemographic factors), it is noteworthy that program characteristics were still significantly associated with children's outcomes on this standardized screening measure.

Examining the data more closely, we were able to identify which program factors and which child outcomes were in fact most responsible for these significant overall relationships. The ECERS creativity subscale on the program measures, and the DIAL-R language subscale on the child measures, accounted for the strongest and most consistent relationships. The creativity subscale assessed the extent to which programs provided a variety of materials for children to manipulate in such areas as art, music and movement, blocks, sand and water, and dramatic play. Having these materials available, in addition to allowing ample time for their use by children, was significantly correlated with motor, conceptual, and language development as measured on the DIAL-R. Program comparisons (Chapter 6) indicated that High/Scope and comparison sites were virtually identical on the creativity subscale. Hence, it is not surprising that children in the two groups did not differ significantly on these DIAL-R subscales.

From the child's perspective, language development was the area most significantly affected by various dimensions of program quality. Overall program quality and language were significantly correlated in the total sample (r = .52, p < .01), as well as in the High/Scope and comparison groups (r = .56 and r = .48, p < .05). In fact, for the sample as a whole, all but one program variable was significantly related to children's language scores on the DIAL-R. These findings emphasized the centrality of the relationship between a wide range of program characteristics and verbal growth in children. Adult-child interaction was clearly important in language development, as evidenced by the substantial relationship of teacher style and sensitivity to language scores. But a program's physical environment—the variety and accessibility of materials—was also key to the development of language skills. Children's verbal abilities grow when they talk about the materials they are using and the actions they are performing with them.

Table 42

PROGRAM OBSERVATIONS CORRELATED WITH CHILDREN'S DIAL-R
SCORES (MEAN DIAL-R SCORES ACROSS CHILDREN IN SAME PROGRAM)

	DIAL-R			
Program Observation Variable	Motor	Concepts	Language	Total
A. Total Sample (*N* = 26)				
ARNETT Total	.03	.25	.53***	.19
ECERS Personal Care	-.07	.10	.08	-.11
ECERS Furnishings	.07	.16	.39**	.09
ECERS Language	.23	.16	.48**	.27*
ECERS Motor	.06	.22	.47**	.20
ECERS Creativity	.51***	.37**	.61****	.34**
ECERS Social	-.09	.04	.38**	.03
ECERS Total	.08	.16	.46***	.16
PIP Phys. Envir.	.05	.11	.56***	.12
PIP Daily Routine	.18	-.01	.32**	.19
PIP Adult-Child	.11	-.01	.32**	.13
PIP Total	.12	.02	.35**	.15
PROGRAM QUALITY (Σ ARNETT, ECERS, PIP)	.24	.19	.52***	.32**
B. High/Scope Sample (*N* = 13)				
ARNETT Total	.13	.26	.35	.30
ECERS Personal Care	.13	.17	-.12	-.17
ECERS Furnishings	.45*	.28	.31	.23
ECERS Language	.39*	.16	.28	.35
ECERS Motor	.22	.03	.20	.13
ECERS Creativity	.71***	.49**	.53**	.52**
ECERS Social	.00	-.04	.29	-.04
ECERS Total	.39*	.11	.49**	.19
PIP Phys. Envir.	.19	.11	.60**	.22
PIP Daily Routine	.07	-.19	.40*	-.01
PIP Adult-Child	.28	-.01	.48**	.18
PIP Total	.20	-.05	.48**	.15
PROGRAM QUALITY (Σ ARNETT, ECERS, PIP)	.12	.18	.56**	.28
C. Comparison Sample (*N*=13)				
ARNETT Total	-.06	.25	.61**	.07
ECERS Personal Care	-.18	.01	.24	.01
ECERS Furnishings	-.16	.06	.42*	-.03
ECERS Language	.13	.17	.54**	.16
ECERS Motor	-.07	.40*	.63***	.22

Table 42 (continued)

PROGRAM OBSERVATIONS CORRELATED WITH CHILDREN'S DIAL-R
SCORES (MEAN DIAL-R SCORES ACROSS CHILDREN IN SAME PROGRAM)

	DIAL-R			
Program Observation Variable	Motor	Concepts	Language	Total
ECERS Creativity	.52**	.34	.65***	.48**
ECERS Social	-.16	.09	.42*	.05
ECERS Total	-.08	.20	.55**	.12
PIP Phys. Envir.	-.05	.10	.53**	.04
PIP Daily Routine	.20	.14	.29	.28
PIP Adult-Child	-.04	.00	.40*	.07
PIP Total	.02	.09	.45*	.13
PROGRAM QUALITY (Σ ARNETT, ECERS, PIP)	.30	.11	.48**	.45*

$^*p < .10.$ $^{**}p < .05.$ $^{***}p < .01.$ $^{****}p < .001.$

Program quality and the COR   Table 43 presents the correlations between
program observation measures and children's ratings on the COR for the
total sample ($N = 26$ programs) and for each group separately ($N = 13$ programs). In the total sample as well as in both groups, there were several
strong positive relationships between program quality subscales and children's
observed behavior. One program factor and two child variables accounted
for most of these strong and consistent positive associations. The program
factor was PIP daily routine, which measured opportunities for children to
plan activities, carry out their ideas, and review what they had done during
the day. PIP daily routine was significantly correlated with five of the six
COR subscales (r ranging from .31, $p < .05$, to .52, $p < .01$). High/Scope
programs were rated significantly higher than comparisons on this central
and distinctive feature of the curriculum (Chapter 6), which in turn may
have accounted for group differences favoring High/Scope children on the
COR.

Children's creative representational skills, and to a lesser extent their
language abilities, were the two COR factors most affected by program
quality. Representation was significantly correlated with the overall index
of program quality ($r = .39$, $p < .05$), as well as with the Arnett and several
ECERS and PIP subscales (r ranging from .32, $p < .05$, to .52, $p < .01$). The
plan-do-review sequence was one important mechanism for enhancing
representational skills. Providing the materials for creative activity and
being open to children's sharing were also avenues for encouraging representational skills. Similarly, language skills were developed when children
discussed their plans and reviewed their activities ($r = .32$, $p < .05$). Adults
played an important role during this process by asking open-ended questions and encouraging children to describe and think about what they were
doing.

Table 43

PROGRAM OBSERVATIONS CORRELATED WITH CHILDREN'S COR RATINGS (MEAN COR SCORES ACROSS CHILDREN IN SAME PROGRAM)

Program Observation Variable	COR Initia-tive	Social Rela-tions	Repre-senta-tion	Lan-guage	Logic & Math	Music & Move-ment	Total
A. Total Sample ($N = 26$)							
ARNETT Total	-.01	.02	.37**	.16	.07	.11	.05
ECERS Personal Care	-.01	.03	.04	.00	-.09	-.04	-.11
ECERS Furnishings	-.25	-.09	.03	-.05	-.04	-.19	-.03
ECERS Language	-.07	.05	.32**	.00	.06	.16	.17
ECERS Motor	-.12	.18	.35**	.43***	.11	.01	.09
ECERS Creativity	-.16	.09	.32**	.14	.20	.01	.10
ECERS Social	-.07	-.13	.08	.00	-.07	-.05	-.06
ECERS Total	-.14	.02	.20	.07	.04	-.02	.04
PIP Phys. Envir.	-.08	-.04	.19	.16	-.05	.06	.03
PIP Daily Routine	.41***	.31**	.52***	.32**	.15	.43***	.36**
PIP Adult-Child	.00	.02	.33**	.38**	.03	.03	.06
PIP Total	-.02	-.02	.25	.33**	.00	.05	.06
PROGRAM QUALITY (Σ ARNETT, ECERS, PIP)	.11	.16	.39**	.13	.03	.02	.14
B. High/Scope Sample ($N = 13$)							
ARNETT Total	.21	-.04	.42*	.26	.27	-.08	.01
ECERS Personal Care	-.27	-.18	-.20	-.15	-.43*	-.26	-.48*
ECERS Furnishings	-.53**	-.13	-.11	-.10	.10	-.40*	-.08
ECERS Language	-.32	-.14	.39*	-.24	.03	-.11	-.12
ECERS Motor	-.18	.09	.19	.46*	.05	-.23	-.04
ECERS Creativity	-.42*	-.15	.36	-.10	.21	-.35	-.19
ECERS Social	-.22	-.29	-.12	-.06	-.05	-.31	-.33
ECERS Total	-.46*	-.19	-.02	-.09	.00	-.40*	-.28
PIP Phys. Envir.	-.25	-.22	-.02	.29	-.06	-.16	-.20
PIP Daily Routine	.56**	.48**	.49**	.51**	-.10	.38	.53**
PIP Adult-Child	-.27	-.13	.40*	.49**	-.02	-.25	-.22
PIP Total	-.25	-.16	.08	.43*	-.05	-.22	-.22
PROGRAM QUALITY (Σ ARNETT, ECERS, PIP)	.14	.13	.48**	.15	.08	.05	.24
C. Comparison Sample ($N = 13$)							
ARNETT Total	-.21	.02	.28	.05	-.02	.26	.06
ECERS Personal Care	.20	.26	.29	.12	.23	.23	.21
ECERS Furnishings	-.08	-.08	.12	-.03	-.13	.00	.01

Table 43 (continued)

PROGRAM OBSERVATIONS CORRELATED WITH CHILDREN'S COR RATINGS
(MEAN COR SCORES ACROSS CHILDREN IN SAME PROGRAM)

	COR						
Program Observation Variable	Initia- tive	Social Rela- tions	Repre- senta- tion	Lan- guage	Logic & Math	Music & Move- ment	Total
ECERS Language	.01	.15	.36	.09	.15	.39*	.36
ECERS Motor	-.11	.25	.35	.42*	.21	.26	.18
ECERS Creativity	-.03	.29	.48**	.29	.23	.32	.29
ECERS Social	.00	-.02	.20	.02	-.07	.16	.09
ECERS Total	-.01	.15	.32	.14	.10	.25	.20
PIP Phys. Envir.	-.02	.07	.30	.12	.00	.23	.17
PIP Daily Routine	.40*	.26	.52**	.39*	.16	.40*	.41*
PIP Adult-Child	.28	.21	.48**	.22	.11	.46*	.37
PIP Total	.15	.12	.39*	.27	.09	.38	.33
PROGRAM QUALITY (Σ ARNETT, ECERS, PIP)	.04	.17	.36	.12	.02	-.05	.11

* $p < .10$. ** $p < .05$. *** $p < .01$.

Despite many significant relationships among subscales, overall program quality was positively but not significantly correlated with the COR total score. This result was due in part to the low sample sizes, but also to some unexpected negative correlations between the program and child subscales in the High/Scope group. Most puzzling was the negative relationship of COR initiative with ECERS furnishings ($r = -.53$, $p < .05$) and creativity ($r = -.42$, $p < .10$). Both of the ECERS scales measure equipment and materials in the classroom, while the COR scale is more a measure of how children use these materials. The negative correlation may reflect instances where programs invest resources in stocking up on supplies without giving corresponding thought to how children use them. In fact, whereas an overabundance of materials may inhibit children's ingenuity and flexibility in manipulating materials in their own ways, a limited but carefully chosen array may spur children to use materials in a wider range of activities.

Agency Factors in Relation to Child Measures

Previous research (e.g., Feeney & Chun, 1985; Whitebook et al., 1989) has looked at how organizational climate affects teachers' attitudes and performance in the classroom. The present study also afforded an opportunity to examine whether these agency factors might play a role in children's development. Table 44 presents the findings regarding the relationship between organizational climate variables and children's measures for the sample as a whole. (Findings for each group—High/Scope and comparison—matched the total pattern and did not differ from one another.) The Table 44 findings can be summarized as follows:

- Both positive and negative aspects of organizational climate were significantly associated with children's development as measured with the COR. Negative, but not positive, aspects of climate were significantly related to the DIAL-R.

- Greater administrative support was associated with higher COR scores ($r = .41$, $p < .01$).

- Higher teacher salaries were associated with higher COR scores ($r = .33$, $p < .05$).

- Greater frustration about working conditions was associated with lower scores on both the COR ($r = -.32$, $p < .05$) and the DIAL-R ($r = -.35$, $p < .05$).

When teachers were supported and better compensated for their work, the children in their programs scored higher on measures of development. The direction of influence cannot be determined from these correlations, but it is reasonable to suggest that teachers who are unhappy in their jobs will devote less energy to program development and children's welfare. By

Table 44

ORGANIZATIONAL CLIMATE CORRELATED WITH CHILD MEASURES
(MEAN DIAL-R AND COR SCORES ACROSS CHILDREN IN SAME PROGRAM),
TOTAL SAMPLE ($N = 26$)

Child Measures	Agency Variables				
	Admin. Support	Salary	Benefits	Job Frustrations	Job Rewards
DIAL-R Motor	.01	-.09	-.04	.07	-.24
DIAL-R Concepts	-.05	-.01	-.01	-.31*	-.13
DIAL-R Language	.09	-.13	-.01	-.30*	-.14
DIAL-R Total	.00	.08	.01	-.35**	.06
COR Initiative	.42***	.44***	-.07	.09	-.05
COR Social Relations	.32**	.11	.15	-.17	-.01
COR Representation	.41***	.11	.15	-.09	-.12
COR Language	.33**	.03	.15	-.19	-.05
COR Logic & Math	-.03	-.01	.02	-.24	-.07
COR Physical Devel.	.32**	.31*	-.01	-.10	.08
COR Total	.41***	.33**	.03	-.32**	-.04

*$p < .10$. **$p < .05$. ***$p < .01$.

contrast, teachers who feel valued and whose own professional development is promoted will in turn offer an enriched learning environment to children. The abilities assessed with the COR—such as taking the initiative and sharing one's experiences—flourish in an open atmosphere. Perhaps teachers working in positive environments feel freer to offer more freedom to the children in their programs.

Teacher and Program Factors in Relation to Child Measures

The final area of analysis was the relationship between teachers' background (education, inservice training, experience) and program quality, on the one hand, and children's development, on the other. Table 45 presents the correlations between these teacher and program factors and children's DIAL-R and COR scores for the total sample ($N = 26$ programs) and for each group separately ($N = 13$ programs). To emphasize the relative contributions of teacher background variables and program quality to children's development, the last column of Table 45 repeats the correlations between overall program quality and child outcomes from Tables 42 and 43.

Table 45 can be summarized as follows:

- *Teachers' formal education* was not significantly associated with either of the child measures. Although formal education was associated with program quality, by itself it did not affect children's development.

- *Teachers' early childhood experience* was positively and significantly associated with children's COR scores. This relationship was found for the sample as a whole ($r = .32$, $p < .05$) and for the High/Scope group ($r = .48$, $p < .05$); the correlation was positive but not significant in the comparison group ($r = .23$). The COR assesses children's interactions with people and materials in a wide variety of learning contexts. Perhaps experience in a good program setting helps teachers to develop the sensitivity and skills for supporting children's exploration and development.

- *Amount of inservice training* was positively and significantly associated with children's DIAL-R scores for the total sample ($r = .39$, $p < .05$), and particularly with concepts ($r = .75$, $p < .01$) and language ($r = .75$, $p < .01$) in the High/Scope group and with motor development ($r = .49$, $p < .05$) in the comparison group. Training may not only sensitize teachers to children's developmental abilities but also encourage them to provide the kinds of experiences necessary for children's motor, conceptual, and language growth. Inservice training was positively and significantly related to COR scores in the High/Scope group only ($r = .48$, $p < .05$). This finding confirms the effectiveness of the curriculum workshops and classroom visits reported by the High/Scope teachers. Focused and intensive inservice training for adults appears to benefit young children, particularly in the development of their social ($r = .41$, $p < .10$), representational ($r = .58$, $p < .05$), and language ($r = .49$, $p < .05$) skills.

Table 45

TEACHER BACKGROUND AND PROGRAM QUALITY CORRELATED
WITH CHILD MEASURES (MEAN DIAL-R AND COR SCORES
ACROSS CHILDREN IN SAME PROGRAM)

Child Measures	Hours of Inservice Training	Years of Formal Education	Years of ECE Experience	Program Quality
A. Total Sample (*N* = 26)				
DIAL-R Motor	.31**	.13	-.03	.24
DIAL-R Concepts	.15	.04	-.17	.19
DIAL-R Language	.18	.03	-.08	.52***
DIAL-R Total	.39**	.17	-.01	.32**
COR Initiative	.00	-.01	.46***	.11
COR Social Relations	.01	.09	.37**	.16
COR Representation	.09	.06	.38**	.39**
COR Language	.13	-.07	.32**	.13
COR Logic & Math	-.02	-.10	.15	.03
COR Physical Devel.	.04	.15	.35**	.02
COR Total	-.01	.02	.32**	.14
B. High/Scope Sample (*N* = 13)				
DIAL-R Motor	.24	.07	.17	.12
DIAL-R Concepts	.75***	.15	-.03	.18
DIAL-R Language	.75***	.06	.02	.56**
DIAL-R Total	.50**	.11	.20	.28
COR Initiative	.24	-.04	.61**	.14
COR Social Relations	.41*	.12	.48**	.13
COR Representation	.58**	.06	.50**	.48**
COR Language	.49**	-.05	.46*	.15
COR Logic & Math	.36	-.09	.21	.08
COR Physical Devel.	.27	.19	.47*	.05
COR Total	.48**	.04	.48**	.24
C. Comparison Sample (*N* = 13)				
DIAL-R Motor	.49**	.33	-.13	.30
DIAL-R Concepts	-.04	.08	-.10	.11
DIAL-R Language	-.08	.23	-.09	.48**
DIAL-R Total	.32	.31	-.08	.45*
COR Initiative	-.14	-.17	.36	.04
COR Social Relations	-.12	-.10	.36	.17
COR Representation	.03	.07	.36	.36
COR Language	.16	-.08	.27	.12
COR Logic & Math	-.06	.05	-.08	.02
COR Physical Devel.	-.17	.10	.24	-.05
COR Total	.01	-.04	.23	.11

* p < .10. ** p < .05. *** p < .01.

- *Program quality* was positively and significantly associated with children's DIAL-R scores for the total sample ($r = .32$, $p < .05$). Program quality was significantly related to COR representation ($r = .39$, $p < .05$) although not to the COR total score. Patterns in each group were similar to one another and to the findings for the sample as a whole. These findings are consistent with the significant relationships between quality and children's development reported and discussed earlier in the chapter.

Given all the other family and demographic influences on children's growth, it is noteworthy that these teacher and program factors were also significant predictors of development. The associations confirm the importance of what happens to teachers *after* they complete their formal schooling. Experience and training are valuable *if* they happen within the context of a well-run program. When these factors are in place—experiential learning through inservice training in a good program environment—teachers can develop as professionals and in turn enhance the development of young children.

Summary of Curriculum Study Results

Group Comparisons on Child Measures

1. High/Scope and comparison children were similar on most preacademic assessments.

2. High/Scope children showed more initiative than comparison children.

- High/Scope children engaged in more complex play than comparison children.

- High/Scope children joined in more program activities than comparison children.

3. High/Scope children had better social relations than comparison children.

- High/Scope children engaged in more social interaction and cooperation with their peers than comparison children.

- High/Scope children were more adept than comparison children at social problem-solving.

4. High/Scope children tended to outscore comparison children on measures of cognitive development.

- High/Scope children tended to be better than comparison children on creative representation and classification (sorting) activities.

- High/Scope children tended to have better language skills than comparison children.

5. High/Scope children were better than comparison children on measures of motor development.

- High/Scope children were better than comparison children at coordinating listening and movement skills.

- High/Scope children were better than comparison children at focusing their physical energies during activities.

6. Comparison children showed no significant advantages over High/Scope children on any of the child assessments.

Program Quality in Relation to Child Measures

7. Access to diverse materials and opportunities for planning and recall were the two dimensions of program quality having the strongest and most consistent relationships with children's development.

- Access to diverse materials for creative manipulation was positively associated with all areas of children's development on standardized screening measures. The equal availability of such materials in High/Scope and comparison programs helped to explain the similar performance of children in both groups.

- Opportunities to plan, carry out, and review activities of their own choosing were positively associated with almost all aspects of children's emotional, social, cognitive, and motor development. This distinguishing feature of the High/Scope plan-do-review sequence helped to explain the significant differences that favored children in the High/Scope group.

8. Children's language and creative representational skills were the two areas most strongly and consistently affected by program quality.

- Language was positively affected by the accessibility of materials and by teacher-child interaction styles. Verbal skills develop when children talk about what and how they are using materials during activities.

- Representation was positively affected by materials and the social context in which they were used. Children benefit from planning constructive activities, carrying them out by manipulating diverse materials, and describing the process afterwards to adults and peers.

Agency Factors in Relation to Child Measures

9. When teachers were supported and reasonably compensated for their work, the children in their programs scored higher on measures of development.

- Higher salaries and administrative support were positively associated with children's development. Abilities such as taking the initiative and sharing one's experiences flourish in an open atmosphere. Perhaps teachers working in positive environments feel freer to offer more freedom to the children in their programs.

- Greater job frustration was negatively associated with children's development. Teachers who are unhappy in their jobs may devote less energy to program development and child welfare.

Teacher and Program Factors in Relation to Child Measures

10. Teachers' formal education was not significantly associated with children's development.

11. Experience, training, and program quality were all significantly associated with children's development.

- Experience was positively and significantly associated with the observational measures of children's development, particularly for the High/Scope group. This finding demonstrates the importance of what happens to teachers after they complete their formal schooling. Experience can be valuable if it is obtained in the context of a well-run program.

- Inservice training was positively and significantly associated with children's development. In both the High/Scope group and the comparison group, more training was associated with higher scores on the developmental screening measure. In the High/Scope group, adult training was associated with better social, representational, and language development in children. Inservice training with an emphasis on experiential learning can create a positive environment in which both adults and children flourish.

- Program quality was positively and significantly associated with children's development, particularly with their language and representational abilities. Given all the additional influences on development, it is noteworthy that program characteristics are nevertheless an important factor in the growth of the young child.

VIII Summary and Implications

The Training of Trainers (ToT) Evaluation investigated the efficacy of the High/Scope model for improving the quality of early childhood programs on a national scale. To address this question, the High/Scope Foundation undertook an ambitious multimethod evaluation that collected anecdotal records from the consultants and 793 participants in 40 ToT projects, surveyed a random sample of 203 endorsed trainers around the country, interviewed and observed highly qualified teachers in 244 High/Scope and 122 non-High/Scope settings, and assessed 97 children in High/Scope and 103 children in comparison programs.

In addition to the particular question about High/Scope's effectiveness in doing training, the study also addressed broader questions about the role of inservice training in improving early childhood program quality and enhancing young children's development: Does inservice training, over and above education and experience, improve a teacher's ability to deliver an appropriate and challenging program to young children? Does this training result in recognizable benefits for the children? And if it is possible to improve program quality and child outcomes, then what have we learned about *how* training can be structured to bring about these positive results?

Overview of Lessons Learned

The study provided a strongly affirmative answer to the first question, Does High/Scope training work? Program sites around the country, separated from the Foundation by both time and distance, were implementing the High/Scope Curriculum at impressive levels of fidelity and quality. High/Scope sites significantly outscored comparison sites on a developmentally based index of program quality. Children in High/Scope programs significantly outscored those in comparison programs on measures of developmental progress.

The research also provided strong evidence for the general assertion that inservice training contributes significantly to program quality and children's development. On-the-job training continues the process of professional development after formal education ceases. On-site learning helps teachers convert experience into improved practice. And better program quality in turn promotes better child development.

Knowing that inservice training can work leads to the final question, How does the early childhood field put this knowledge into practice? Clearly, the first step is to ensure that there are enough qualified people to provide inservice training on a national scale. Second, the challenge is to guarantee that the ingredients of successful training are present in the services they deliver to adult practitioners. And third, our ultimate goal is to guarantee that the resulting program practices are truly beneficial to young children.

This evaluation demonstrated that the High/Scope Curriculum and training process constitute one way to achieve these results. The dissemination model that began with High/Scope consultants and endorsed trainers was strong enough to link teachers to the chain. And the High/Scope Curriculum implemented by these teachers was in turn powerful enough to enhance the development of young children and thus complete the final link in the dissemination chain. The High/Scope Perry Preschool study (Beruetta-Clement et al., 1984) and Curriculum Comparison study (Schweinhart et al., 1986) showed that the High/Scope Curriculum could work on a closely monitored local level. The current study showed that the Foundation's model for training and curriculum implementation could be successfully mounted on a national scale. We now know that we have long-term effects and that we have widespread effects; future follow-up will determine if High/Scope can deliver effects that are both long-lasting and broad in their impact.

We also have evidence that this process can achieve the numbers necessary to improve program quality on a national scale. The multiplicative effect of each project—which links one High/Scope consultant to two dozen trainers to 600 teachers—is substantial. As of 1991, 1,075 endorsed High/Scope trainers had trained an estimated 26,000 teachers working with over a quarter of a million children annually in 13,000 programs. Nearly 6,000 (45 percent) of these programs were rated by their trainers as reaching demonstration-level quality. To date, High/Scope has been able to reach 6 percent of potential early childhood training professionals overall, including 12.5 percent of those serving low-income children. As impressive as these numbers are, the need to prepare qualified early childhood staff is even greater. We know the need, and now we know how to go about meeting it.

This final chapter reviews the evidence behind these assertions and explores their implications for training and curriculum development. It begins with a summary of results, presenting the outcomes for each link in the dissemination chain and insights into why the process was successful. The report concludes with the lessons this model teaches us about meeting the growing challenges of early childhood education:

- *For trainers:* Preparing a national cadre of early childhood trainers

- *For teachers:* Providing inservice training that brings about real changes in teaching practices

- *For children:* Implementing a curriculum that embodies the principles of good quality and enhances the development of young children

Summary of Results

The Evidence for Achieving Program Quality

Both High/Scope and comparison settings offered high-quality programs. But there were significant differences, and the majority of them favored High/Scope. Comparison programs were better at supporting gross-motor development. High/Scope programs were better at organizing the environment, encouraging independent thought and action, and using adult-child interaction to promote reasoning and language skills.

It is important to remember that the comparison group was itself selected from a pool of good early childhood programs. Overall, teachers in the study appeared to represent the top 20 percent of early childhood practitioners, in terms of education and experience. Programs in both groups provided safe and well-equipped physical environments, with nurturing adults who were sensitive to children's needs. Still, the majority of significant program-quality comparisons favored High/Scope sites.

The single area in which comparison programs excelled was in promoting children's gross-motor development. They provided more equipment, space, and time for large-muscle activities. Both the equipment and the activities were used to help children develop other skills, such as building and dramatic play. It is possible that many early childhood programs choose to devote more of their resources to the area of motor development. But there is also the implication that High/Scope, which has been implementing a successful music and movement curriculum, might consider broadening its focus to devote more time and materials to other areas of physical growth.

In other domains, however, High/Scope programs were rated consistently better than comparison programs. Moreover, these differences were all in keeping with the central features of the Curriculum model regarding room arrangement, the plan-do-review sequence, and the role of adults in supporting children's learning. In High/Scope settings the rooms were organized and labeled to guarantee the accessibility of materials and promote children's greater independence, self-care, initiation, and multicultural awareness. Children in High/Scope programs were more often encouraged to choose activities based on their own interests, carry out plans in accordance with their developmental levels, and reflect on their actions and experiences through creative representation and communication. High/Scope teachers were better than comparison teachers at observing and extending children's play by using open-ended questions to promote problem-solving and verbal skills.

Teachers' formal education, inservice training, and experience were *all* highly significant predictors of program quality.

There is currently an increasing demand for and a growing shortage of qualified early childhood staff. This study's results are encouraging in suggesting several avenues for improving provider skills. Clearly, formal education continues to be an effective method for preparing practitioners. Compared with teachers without college degrees, those with college degrees implemented programs that provided better physical, socioemotional, and cognitive environments for young children. Teachers with early childhood degrees were better than those without specialized coursework at providing materials to develop children's creative and social skills.

But for those already in the workplace and those unable to consider extended formal education, experience obtained in conjunction with ongoing inservice training can also result in developmentally appropriate teaching practices. Other studies (e.g., Ruopp et al., 1979; Whitebook et al., 1989) have found that experience by itself does not result in good caregiving practices. But this study shows that experience, in the context of a good program environment and systematic ongoing training, can provide the role models and support needed for professional development.

The results suggest not only *how* to improve teaching skills, but also *whom* to target in a national strategy to upgrade program quality. If the study sample represented on average the top 20 percent of early childhood teachers, then how do we reach the other 80 percent of the field? One effective strategy may indeed be to focus training efforts at the upper end, thereby creating a good learning environment within which less experienced cohorts of providers can be trained. This approach was used successfully, for example, in the Head Start Leadership Training Program (Bloom et al., 1991). In this pilot initiative, college-educated directors and head teachers were seen as the gateway to improving program quality as a whole. Results showed that an intensive inservice training course for 31 individuals in leadership positions in fact improved program quality among the teachers they supervised. The ToT study replicated these findings on a larger scale and down another level. In addition to preparing leaders at the endorsed trainer level, the High/Scope model created potential leaders at the teacher level. Providing inservice training to experienced teachers, and then encouraging them to act as mentors toward less experienced staff, acknowledges their potential leadership role in improving the quality of early childhood programs.

Organizational climate was significantly associated with program quality. Teachers characterized the organizational climate in High/Scope agencies as being significantly better than that in comparison agencies.

Across all programs, the better the working environment for adults, the better the program quality for children. Significant factors included higher salaries, better benefit-options, absence of workplace frustrations, and higher levels of administrative support. High/Scope teachers rated their administrators as being more supportive than did comparison teachers. In addition to providing more training opportunities, High/Scope agencies also encouraged more sharing among staff members. The ratings confirmed anecdotal reports that teamwork among staff members improved greatly after inservice training was instituted. Teachers saw all these workplace features as being important to organizational climate in general and to program development in particular. They implemented better programs when they felt that their agencies provided for their operational and professional needs.

These results were certainly consistent with other research (e.g., Bloom, 1988; Whitebook et al., 1989) and with the current emphasis of the National Association for the Education of Young Children on professional development and recognition for early childhood practitioners (Bredekamp & Willer, 1992). But it is not enough to simply state that teachers of young children should have more education, higher salaries, and better inservice training. The field needs empirical evidence that these factors actually contribute to program quality and children's development. The ToT Evaluation adds to the growing body of evidence that enhancing training and working conditions for adults serves to benefit children too.

The Evidence for Promoting Children's Development

Children in High/Scope programs outscored those in comparison programs on measures of emotional, social, cognitive, and motor de-

velopment. Comparison children showed no significant advantages over High/Scope children on any of the child assessments.

Observations and, to a much lesser extent, a screening test indicated that children in High/Scope programs were developmentally ahead of their peers on several dimensions. These results were consistent with systematic observations conducted independently in the United Kingdom (Berry & Sylva, 1987) and with anecdotal accounts offered by candidates and teachers in ToT projects. High/Scope children showed more initiative by engaging in more complex play and joining in more group activities. They also demonstrated more social interaction with peers and were more adept at social problem-solving. Children in High/Scope settings also tended to be better in certain cognitive areas, including creative representation, classification, and language skills. The High/Scope group was better at music and movement skills, an area of curriculum focus. And the High/Scope children were better at focusing their physical energies during activities, perhaps as a result of the opportunities for sustained attention in the plan-do-review sequence.

Children's access to diverse materials and their opportunities for planning and recall were the two dimensions of program quality having the strongest and most-consistent relationships with child measures.

Access to diverse materials for creative manipulation was positively associated with all areas of children's development on standardized screening measures. The equal availability of such materials in both High/Scope and comparison programs helped to explain the similar performance of children in both groups. Opportunities to plan, carry out, and review activities of their own choosing were positively associated with almost all aspects of children's emotional, social, cognitive, and motor development. This distinguishing feature of the High/Scope plan-do-review sequence helped to explain the significant developmental differences that favored children in the High/Scope group.

Children's language and creative-representation skills were the two areas of development most strongly and consistently affected by program quality.

Language was positively affected by the accessibility of materials and by teacher-child interaction styles. Verbal skills develop when children talk about what and how they are using materials during activities. Creative representation was positively affected by materials and the social context in which they were used. Children benefit from planning constructive activities, carrying them out by manipulating diverse materials, and describing or demonstrating the process to adults and peers.

Teachers' experience, teachers' training, and program quality were all significant predictors of children's development. Teachers' formal education was not significantly associated with children's development.

These findings again demonstrate the importance of what happens to teachers after or instead of formal schooling. Education alone, while one determinant of program quality, does not extend its influence directly to children's development. However, experience can be valuable if it is obtained in the context of a well-run program. And inservice training, with an emphasis on experiential learning, can create a positive environment in which both adults and children flourish.

The Evidence for Mounting Successful Training Strategies

A systematic dissemination model can produce an impressive number of qualified trainers. The vast majority of ToT candidates became endorsed High/Scope trainers. Most applied their skills, typically spending 8 hours a week training lead teachers and aides in 12 classrooms.

Over 80 percent of ToT candidates were endorsed at the end of their projects. Over 80 percent of these endorsed trainers continued to conduct High/Scope training during the succeeding years, each working with approximately 25 teachers. Based on these figures, the 1,075 trainers endorsed as of 1991 have trained an estimated 26,000 early childhood teachers and improved the developmental quality of programs for over a quarter of a million children annually. Thus the investment in training paid off and will continue to generate returns. Financial contributions—from sponsoring agencies, public funding sources, and private foundations—resulted in a corps of skilled early childhood trainers with long-term commitments to the field.

Their training activities generally consisted of one large-group presentation each year to introduce the curriculum, monthly hands-on workshops with small groups of staff members, monthly visits to conduct observation and feedback, and informal visits to each classroom three times a month. A typical teacher received more than a year and a half of training in the High/Scope Curriculum. Trainers considered that 45 percent of the classrooms they worked in had reached demonstration-level quality. Based on the figures in the preceding paragraph, there are an estimated 13,000 programs nationwide using the High/Scope framework, and 6,000 of these are implementing the curriculum at notably high levels.

An intensive program that combines a theoretical framework with hands-on practice can develop training skills and establish a professional training network.

ToT made trainers conversant in the basic elements of a developmental curriculum. It enhanced their ability to transfer this curriculum to teachers by conducting workshops that actively involved adults. The project taught them observation/feedback techniques to monitor and improve program implementation. And ToT armed trainers with effective strategies for overcoming the barriers to organizational change. Candidates found that their immersion in training was valuable for promoting internalization and renewing their commitment to the early childhood field. Additionally, ToT broadened candidates' awareness of the field's potential reach. Trainers established networks (for moral and technical support) spanning local, state, and regional domains. Contact with High/Scope introduced endorsed trainers to a national and international movement for improving training and quality in early childhood programs.

Agencies with the interest and resources will make a commitment to providing inservice training. High/Scope agencies provided significantly more inservice training for teachers than comparison agencies did. High/Scope training featured the consistency of an in-house staff-development specialist, a focus on curriculum and teaching issues, and active participation by teachers.

The large majority of agencies in both groups provided inservice training: 94 percent for High/Scope and 84 percent for comparison sites. However, significant differences favored High/Scope in both the amount and the type of professional development options available. High/Scope agencies emphasized the importance of inservice training by making it a requirement. Teachers in High/Scope programs had more workshops and classroom visits by in-house trainers. Their training more often covered curriculum and teaching issues. Typical practice in the field has been for an agency to invite a series of unrelated outside experts to lead presentations. But the continuity and consistency of having a within-agency consultant allow an agency's teachers to develop a coherent system of program practices. They can build incrementally on their skills, translate workshop ideas into practice, and refine implementation by observing the results of their activities. This model is more likely to produce real and lasting changes in program quality. In fact, the High/Scope teachers described themselves as significantly more likely than comparisons to change their teaching practices based on inservice training experiences.

Training techniques that are successful with teachers can be adapted for parents. High/Scope workshops, observations, and classroom participation reportedly improved parents' understanding of children's development.

The evaluation was not able to include a quantitative assessment of parental attitudes and behaviors. However, anecdotal evidence from trainers and teachers suggested that parents can embrace and learn from the High/Scope approach toward working with adults and children. Parents, some of whom were initially skeptical, came to appreciate the importance of play in children's learning. Their emphasis on "traditional academics" decreased. In the home environment, parents expanded the range of materials and choices available to their children. They used open-ended conversational strategies more often and appeared to find greater enjoyment in their relationships with their children.

Implications

Preparing a National Cadre of Early Childhood Trainers

Systematic leadership training can prepare a trainers' corps, national in scope, capable of disseminating to teaching staff a body of early childhood theory and practice.

A national investment in training will result in improved program practices and enhanced child outcomes on an expanding scale. The dissemination chain will expand at a ratio of 1 trainer to 25 teachers serving 250 children per year. There are currently 7.3 million 3- and 4-year-olds in the United States, with 4.5 million (61.4 percent) of them in early childhood programs. Based on the 1 to 25 trainer-teacher ratio, we would need to prepare a national corps of 18,000 trainers to reach every teacher and every child enrolled in a program. Furthermore, if all 1.6 million poor 3- and 4-year-olds were served in Head Start or other subsidized programs, a corps of 6,400 trainers could insure that high-quality programs produced a return on the public investment.

Methods for preparing a trainers' corps can be effective if they embody the principles of active learning for adults.

To maintain momentum along the transmission chain, preparation of those at the starting point must be powerful enough to carry through both time and distance. To jump-start the transmission process, members of the trainers' corps should receive the following: an intense immersion in the training process, opportunities to integrate developmental theory and practice into a coherent framework, a dual emphasis on adult learning and children's development, opportunities to network and appreciate one another's significance as part of a larger (inter)national initiative, strategies for addressing the organizational change process, and follow-up training to continue the process of learning and disseminating the curriculum (i.e., inservice for the trainers).

Agencies can enhance the work of corps members by providing them with organizational support.

Administrative support is a crucial component in the dynamics of organizational change. Effective support is characterized by the following qualities: institutional commitment to the professional development of teaching staff through ongoing inservice training; resources to maintain a trainer as a member of the in-house staff-development team, to provide continuity and consistency in training; and job definition that includes training responsibilities as an explicit role. Trainers may fulfill other administrative or teaching responsibilities, as long as a significant portion of their work time is specifically allocated to training activities.

Providing Inservice Training That Improves Teaching Practices

Inservice training can make a good program even better.

Good programs provide safe and well-equipped physical environments monitored by nurturing adults. But better programs elaborate this physical and interpersonal environment. In better programs, inservice training results in children having improved access to materials, more opportunities to exercise choice, and extended sequences for carrying out and reviewing self-initiated activities. Also, enhanced observational and questioning skills on the part of adults support children's reasoning and language development.

Inservice training, as a supplement to education or experience, is an effective option for further improving program quality.

To effectively use all the mechanisms at our disposal, we must consider how varying combinations of education, experience, and training can interact to produce the best early childhood teachers. Regardless of a teacher's background, ongoing inservice training for adults can make a difference in the quality of programs for young children. Although *formal education* enhances a teacher's ability to deliver a high-quality program, inservice training can promote additional skills, even for caregivers who have earned higher education degrees. *Experience* alone may not produce a well-qualified teacher, but experience together with systematic inservice training can result in the professional development of early childhood staff. *Inservice training* targeted at top-level teachers is an effective strategy for upgrading professional skills at all staff levels. Experienced teachers who receive training can establish good learning environments and act as mentors for their less experienced colleagues.

Inservice training can result in improved practices if teachers are engaged in participatory, active learning experiences.

To achieve the maximum benefits for early childhood teachers and caregivers, resources earmarked for inservice training must be invested wisely. Inservice training is most effective when it is characterized by the following components: workshops presented by in-house trainers, with an emphasis on active participation by adults; specific coverage of curriculum issues and teaching practices; classroom visits to observe and give feedback to teachers as they turn ideas into practice; and follow-up sessions that encourage staff to share problems and successful implementation strategies.

Implementing Programs That Enhance the Development of Young Children

Children's development is enhanced by programs that provide access to diverse materials and offer opportunities for planning and recall.

Empirical evidence gives meaning to the statement that high-quality programs offer children developmentally appropriate experiences. We can now define at least two components of program quality that have clear implications for young children's development. First, high-quality programs provide children with ready access to a *broad range of creative materials.* Children benefit when they are encouraged to manipulate diverse materials in activities of their own choosing. Second, high-quality programs provide opportunities for children to *plan, carry out,* and *review* their activities in a supportive context. This sequence promotes children's independent problem solving, social cooperation, and language development.

Children's development is enhanced by programs that also support adult development.

When agencies make a commitment to teachers through tangible rewards and ongoing professional development, teachers make a commitment to children. Teachers who are given the freedom to learn experientially extend this same freedom to the children in their programs. Active learning holds equal import for the professional development of adults and the early development of young children. Lessons learned actively are lessons that last.

Discourse about early childhood programs is no longer limited to issues of availability and access. Program quality is now a permanent fixture in the national debate. Developing appropriate curriculum models and preparing staff to deliver their essential ingredients are the keys to achieving the standards inherent in high-quality programs. This study has contributed to our understanding of what defines program quality. And most important, the research has documented the viability of systematic and coherent inservice training for disseminating quality throughout the early childhood community.

It is now up to everyone in the field—classroom teachers, home day care providers, parents, agency administrators, and policymakers from the local to the national level—to convert these lessons into action. We know that inservice training can work on a large scale, and we know what elements are crucial to making it work at the individual-program level. If we are concerned about the professional development of a growing segment of our labor force, and if we are concerned about the quality of the services they deliver to our nation's young children, then we must find the resources to invest in training for quality.

References

Arnett, J. (1989). Teacher's Global Rating Scale. In M. Whitebook, C. Howes, & D. Phillips, *Final report of the National Day Care Staffing Study* (pp. 25–26, 88–94). Oakland, CA: Child Care Employee Project.

Barnett, W. S. (1985). *The Perry Preschool program and its long-term effects: A benefit-cost analysis.* Ypsilanti, MI: High/Scope Press.

Benham, N., Miller, T., & Kontos, S. (1988). Pinpointing staff training needs in child care centers. *Young Children, 43*(4), 9–16.

Berruetta-Clement, J. R., Schweinhart, L. J., Barnett, W. S., Epstein, A. S., & Weikart, D. P. (1984). *Changed lives: The effects of the Perry Preschool program on youths through age 19* (Monographs of the High/Scope Educational Research Foundation, 8). Ypsilanti, MI: High/Scope Press.

Berry, C., & Sylva, K. (1987). *The plan-do-review cycle in High/Scope: Its effects on children and staff.* Oxford: Department of Social and Administrative Studies, University of Oxford.

Bloom, P. J. (1988). Factors influencing overall job satisfaction and organizational commitment in early childhood work environments. *Journal of Research in Childhood Education, 3,* 107–122.

Bloom, P. J., Sheerer, M., Richard, N., & Britz, J. (1991). *The Head Start Leadership Training Program.* Evanston, IL: The Early Childhood Professional Development Project, National-Louis University.

Bredekamp, S. (Ed.). (1987). *Developmentally appropriate practice in early childhood programs serving children from birth through age 8.* Washington, DC: National Association for the Education of Young Children.

Bredekamp, S., & Willer, B. (1992, March). Of ladders and lattices, cores and cones: Conceptualizing an early childhood professional development system. *Young Children, 47*(3), 47–50.

Caldwell, B., & Hilliard, A. (1985). *What is quality child care?* Washington, DC: National Association for the Education of Young Children.

Carnegie Foundation for the Advancement of Teaching. (1991). *National survey of kindergarten teachers.* New York, NY: Author.

Committee for Economic Development. (1985). *Investing in our children.* New York, NY: Author.

Epstein, A. S., Morgan, G., Curry, N., Endsley, R.C., Bradbard, M. R., & Rashid, H. M. (1985). *Quality in early childhood programs: Four perspectives.* Ypsilanti, MI: High/Scope Press.

Feeney, S., & Chun, R. (1985). Effective teachers of young children. *Young Children, 41*(1), 47–52.

Fenichel, E., & Eggbear, L. (1990). *Preparing practitioners to work with infants, toddlers, and their families.* Arlington, VA: National Center for Clinical Infant Programs, TASK Project.

Frede, E., & Barnett, W. S. (1992). Developmentally appropriate public school preschool: A study of implementation of the High/Scope Curriculum and its effects on disadvantaged children's skills at first grade. *Early Childhood Research Quarterly, 7*(4), 483–499.

Gowen, J. W. (1987). Facilitating play skills: Efficacy of a staff development program. *Early Childhood Research Quarterly, 2,* 55–66.

Greenman, J. T. (1984). Program development and models of consultation. In J. Greenman & R. Fuque (Eds.), *Making day care better: Training, evaluation, and the process of change* (pp. 202–226). New York, NY: Teachers College Press.

Harms, T., & Clifford, R. (1980). *The Early Childhood Environment Rating Scale.* New York, NY: Teachers College Press.

High/Scope Educational Research Foundation. (1989). *Program Implementation Profile manual.* Ypsilanti, MI: High/Scope Press.

High/Scope Educational Research Foundation. (1992). *High/Scope Child Observation Record (COR) for Ages 2½–6.* Ypsilanti, MI: High/Scope Press.

Hohmann, M., Banet, B., & Weikart, D. (1979). *Young children in action: A manual for preschool educators.* Ypsilanti, MI: High/Scope Press.

Hohmann, M., & Weikart, D. (in press). *Young children in action* (2d ed., rev. and exp.). Ypsilanti, MI: High/Scope Press.

Jones, E. (1984). Training individuals: In the classroom and out. In J. Greenman & R. Fuqua (Eds.), *Making day care better: Training, evaluation, and the process of change.* New York, NY: Teachers College Press.

Jones, E. (1986). Perspectives on teacher education: Some relations between theory and practice. In L. Katz & K. Steiner (Eds.), *Current topics in early childhood education* (Vol. 6, pp. 123–141). Norwood, NJ: Ablex.

Kahn, A. J., & Kamerman, S. B. (1987). *Child care: Facing the hard choices.* Dover, MA: Auburn House.

Katz, L. (1979). *Helping others learn to teach.* Urbana, IL: ERIC #181.

Katz, L. (1984). The education of preprimary teachers. In L. Katz, P. Wagemaker, & K. Steiner (Eds.), *Current topics in early childhood education* (Vol. 5, pp. 209–227). Norwood, NJ: Ablex.

Knowles, M. S. (1984). Adult learning theory and practice. In L. Nadler (Ed.), *The handbook of human resource development.* New York, NY: Wiley-Interscience.

Knox, A. (1977). *Adult development and learning.* San Francisco, CA: Jossey-Bass.

Kontos, S., & Stevens, R. (1985). High quality child care: Does your center measure up? *Young Children, 40*(2), 5–9.

Larner, M., & Schweinhart, L. (1991, Winter). Focusing in on the teacher trainer: The High/Scope Registry survey. *High/Scope ReSource,* pp. 1, 10–16.

Lombardi, J. (1989). New directions for CDA: Deciding what it means for your program. *Child Care Information Exchange, 70,* 41–43.

Mardell-Czudnowski, C., & Goldenberg, D. S. (1990). *Developmental Indicators for the Assessment of Learning—Revised.* Circle Pines, MN: American Guidance Service, Inc.

Mitchell, A. (1988). *The public school early childhood study.* New York: Bank Street College of Education.

Moore, E., & Smith, T. (1987). *The High/Scope training program one year on.* Oxford: Department of Social and Administrative Studies, University of Oxford.

Morgan, G. (1987). *The national state of child care regulation, 1986.* Watertown, MA: Work/Family Directions, Inc.

National Association for the Education of Young Children. (1984a). *Accreditation criteria and procedures of the National Academy of Early Childhood Programs.* Washington, DC: Author.

National Association for the Education of Young Children. (1984b). *NAEYC position statement on nomenclature, salaries, benefits, and the status of the early childhood profession.* Washington, DC: Author.

National Center for Children in Poverty. (1990). *Five million children: A statistical profile of our poorest young citizens.* New York: Author, Columbia University.

Olson, L. (1990, December 12). Teaching our teachers. *Education Week,* pp. 11–26.

Phillips, D. A. (Ed.). (1987). *Quality in child care: What does research tell us?* Washington, DC: National Association for the Education of Young Children.

Powell, D. R., & Stremmel, A. J. (1989). The relation of early childhood training and experience to the professional development of child care workers. *Early Childhood Research Quarterly, 4,* 339–355.

Rogers, D. L., Waller, C. B., & Perrin, M. S. (1987). Learning more about what makes a good teacher through collaborative research in the classroom. *Young Children, 42*(4), 202–226.

Ruopp, R., Travers, J., Glantz, F., Coelen, C., & Smith, A. (1979). *Children at the center.* Cambridge, MA: Abt Associates.

Schweinhart, L. J. (1985). *Early childhood development programs in the eighties: The national picture.* Ypsilanti, MI: High/Scope Press.

Schweinhart, L. J., McNair, S., Barnes, H., & Larner, M. (1991). *Observing young children in action to assess their development: The High/Scope Child Observation Record study* (Final Report). Ypsilanti, MI: Research Division, High/Scope Educational Research Foundation.

Schweinhart, L. J., Weikart, D. P., & Larner, M. B. (1986). Consequences of three preschool curriculum models through age 15. *Early Childhood Research Quarterly, 1,* 15–45.

Snider, M. H., & Fu, V. (1990). The effects of specialized education and job experience on early childhood teachers' knowledge of developmentally appropriate practice. *Early Childhood Research Quarterly, 5,* 69–78.

Sylva, K., Smith, T., & Moore, E. (1986). *Monitoring the High/Scope training program: 1984–85.* Oxford: Department of Social and Administrative Studies, University of Oxford.

Whitebook, M., Howes, C., Darrah, R., & Friedman, J. (1982). Caring for the caregivers: Staff burnout in child care. In L. G. Katz (Ed.), *Current topics in early childhood education* (Vol. 4, pp. 211–235). Norwood, NJ: Ablex.

Whitebook, M., Howes, C., & Phillips, D. (1989). *Final report of the National Child Care Staffing Study.* Oakland, CA: Child Care Employee Project.

Whitebook, M., Howes, C., & Phillips, D. (1990). *Who cares? Child care teachers and the quality of care in America.* Oakland, CA: Child Care Employee Project.

Willer, B., Hofferth, S. L., Kisker, E. E., Divine-Hawkins, P., Farquhar, E., & Glantz, F. (1991). *The demand and supply of child care in 1990.* Washington, DC: National Association for the Education of Young Children.

Willer, B., & Johnson, L. C. (1989). *The crisis is real: Demographics on the problems of recruiting and retaining early childhood staff.* Washington, DC: National Association for the Education of Young Children.

Zigler, E. F., & Lang, M. E. (1991). *Child care choices: Balancing the needs of children, families, and society.* New York: The Free Press.